JAM, JELLY
AND MARMALADE

Edible

Series Editor: Andrew F. Smith

EDIBLE is a revolutionary series of books dedicated to food and drink that explores the rich history of cuisine. Each book reveals the global history and culture of one type of food or beverage.

Already published

Apple Erika Janik, *Avocado* Jeff Miller, *Banana* Lorna Piatti-Farnell, *Barbecue* Jonathan Deutsch and Megan J. Elias, *Beans* Nathalie Rachel Morris, *Beef* Lorna Piatti-Farnell, *Beer* Gavin D. Smith, *Berries* Heather Arndt Anderson, *Biscuits and Cookies* Anastasia Edwards, *Brandy* Becky Sue Epstein, *Bread* William Rubel, *Cabbage* Meg Muckenhoupt, *Cake* Nicola Humble, *Caviar* Nichola Fletcher, *Champagne* Becky Sue Epstein, *Cheese* Andrew Dalby, *Chillies* Heather Arndt Anderson, *Chocolate* Sarah Moss and Alexander Badenoch, *Cocktails* Joseph M. Carlin, *Coffee* Jonathan Morris, *Corn* Michael Owen Jones, *Curry* Colleen Taylor Sen, *Dates* Nawal Nasrallah, *Doughnut* Heather Delancey Hunwick, *Dumplings* Barbara Gallani, *Edible Flowers* Constance L. Kirker and Mary Newman, *Eggs* Diane Toops, *Fats* Michelle Phillipov, *Figs* David C. Sutton, *Foie Gras* Norman Kolpas, *Game* Paula Young Lee, *Gin* Lesley Jacobs Solmonson, *Hamburger* Andrew F. Smith, *Herbs* Gary Allen, *Herring* Kathy Hunt, *Honey* Lucy M. Long, *Hot Dog* Bruce Kraig, *Ice Cream* Laura B. Weiss, *Jam, Jelly and Marmalade* Sarah B. Hood, *Lamb* Brian Yarvin, *Lemon* Toby Sonneman, *Lobster* Elisabeth Townsend, *Melon* Sylvia Lovegren, *Milk* Hannah Velten, *Moonshine* Kevin R. Kosar, *Mushroom* Cynthia D. Bertelsen, *Mustard* Demet Güzey, *Nuts* Ken Albala, *Offal* Nina Edwards, *Olive* Fabrizia Lanza, *Onions and Garlic* Martha Jay, *Oranges* Clarissa Hyman, *Oyster* Carolyn Tillie, *Pancake* Ken Albala, *Pasta and Noodles* Kantha Shelke, *Pickles* Jan Davison, *Pie* Janet Clarkson, *Pineapple* Kaori O'Connor, *Pizza* Carol Helstosky, *Pomegranate* Damien Stone, *Pork* Katharine M. Rogers, *Potato* Andrew F. Smith, *Pudding* Jeri Quinzio, *Rice* Renee Marton, *Rum* Richard Foss, *Saffron* Ramin Ganeshram, *Salad* Judith Weinraub, *Salmon* Nicolaas Mink, *Sandwich* Bee Wilson, *Sauces* Maryann Tebben, *Sausage* Gary Allen, *Seaweed* Kaori O'Connor, *Shrimp* Yvette Florio Lane, *Soup* Janet Clarkson, *Spices* Fred Czarra, *Sugar* Andrew F. Smith, *Sweets and Candy* Laura Mason, *Tea* Helen Saberi, *Tequila* Ian Williams, *Tomato* Clarissa Hyman, *Truffle* Zachary Nowak, *Vanilla* Rosa Abreu-Runkel, *Vodka* Patricia Herlihy, *Water* Ian Miller, *Whiskey* Kevin R. Kosar, *Wine* Marc Millon, *Yoghurt* June Hersh

Jam, Jelly and Marmalade

A Global History

Sarah B. Hood

REAKTION BOOKS

To my sister Alexandra and my brother John, and their children Tara and Alex, with love and thanks for putting up with me for all these years.

Published by Reaktion Books Ltd
Unit 32, Waterside
44–48 Wharf Road
London N1 7UX, UK
www.reaktionbooks.co.uk

First published 2021
Copyright © Sarah B. Hood 2021

Printed and bound in India by Replika Press Pvt. Ltd

A catalogue record for this book is available from the British Library

ISBN 978 1 78914 389 8

Contents

I

Preserving Traditions

When you open a jar of jam, jelly or marmalade, what's inside? First, the aroma: an intense waft of fresh raspberries, oranges or plums. Then, translucency and colour: brilliant gold, bright scarlet or deep indigo. Next, a pleasing gel, perhaps mixed with luscious fruit pieces. Finally, the sweet and tangy flavour melting on your tongue.

What else? A 2010 academic survey of Americans who make their own preserves showed how strongly people value the potent associations sealed along with the fruit.[1] The survey respondents talked about how 'putting up', or canning, preserves made them feel a connection to older family members, to their forebears and to past cultures. Preserves also have a comforting quality: in their earliest incarnations, they were generally valued for their medicinal properties, and they continued routinely to be fed to invalids well into the nineteenth century.

Every jar of fruit preserves also contains a small miracle: a batch of fruit that ought to have mouldered away months ago, still as delectable as when it was harvested. Chemically speaking, the process is so complex that it seems surprising that anyone managed to figure it out. Nonetheless, human ingenuity, combined with lifetimes of observation, and trial and error, unlocked the secret many centuries ago. Essentially,

Jelly jars on display at Tangled Garden in Grand-Pré, Nova Scotia, Canada.

enabling fruit to gel requires three elements in a fairly specific balance: pectin, sugar and acid.

Pectin is a water-soluble polysaccharide (a carbohydrate) that occurs naturally in plants. When heated in liquid containing sugar, it forms polymer chains that support the structure of the mass it is contained in; in other words, it gels. Citrus fruits, quinces, apples, gooseberries and plums contain a lot. In raspberries, it occurs in the seeds. Pears, blueberries, bananas and many other fruits are weak in pectin; to these, extra pectin can be added.

Powdered or liquid commercial pectin is usually derived from apples or oranges. Some older recipes call for the addition of juice from apples or another pectin-rich fruit to improve the set of a preserve made with low-pectin ingredients. To reduce the amount of sugar needed to make jam, modern manufacturers have developed something called 'low-methoxyl pectin', which uses added calcium to form bridges that link the pectins together.

The classic ratio of sugar to fruit in jams and jellies is 1:1, including the sugar already present in the fruit. To modern, sugar-averse consumers, this seems like a lot, but commercial producers have frequently used much more, as sugar has often been cheaper than fruit. Also, besides imparting a bright, jewel-like colour and a firm gel, sugar plays an important role in preserving the fruit, retarding the growth of moulds and fungi after the jar is opened. Beet sugar acts in the same way as cane sugar. Honey has good preservative qualities, but does not offer the same look and texture. Corn syrup can be used, but only in combination with sugar.

In order to gel, jams, jellies and marmalades must have a low pH value, around 3.0, which signifies a fairly high level of acid (lower pH equals higher acid level). As it happens, the classic jam fruits, like apples, citrus fruits, quince, grapes and many berries, fall close to this level. Lemon and lime juice, which can be as low as 2.0, are often used to correct the acid level of preserves. A low-pH (or high-acid) environment is inhospitable to foodborne pathogens; in fact, *Clostridium botulinum*, the bacterium that causes potentially fatal botulism poisoning, cannot grow below a pH of 4.6. It's nice to know that if jam, jelly or marmalade has set correctly by natural means, it cannot harbour botulism. Heating a fruit preserve to boiling point further kills potential pathogens, and when hot preserves have been sealed inside a sterile glass or ceramic container they will remain shelf-stable for two or more years.

It was not until the twentieth century that science gained the tools to explain in detail these principles, which had been practised around the world since ancient times. The first prototypes of our jams, jellies and marmalades were being made so long ago that their origin has never been written down. The shared knowledge of fruit preserving, passed down over centuries, is a vital link to our human past.

2

Roman and Persian Contributions

How long ago did some early human think of mixing up fruit or berries with a little honey, and noticed that it not only tasted better but resisted spoilage? The first sweet preserves were probably created to make fruit last beyond its usual short lifespan, but people evidently began to seek out the concentrated flavours of these long-lasting foods for their own sake as well.

By the time of ancient Rome, people had probably been mixing up various concoctions of dried and sweetened fruit for quite a while. We know from the collection of culinary writings called *Apicius* or *De re coquinaria* (On Cooking) that the Romans knew how to preserve quinces by packing them in a sealed pot with honey and the thick grape syrup they called *defrutum*. Honey was the most common sweetener for fruit preserves across the ancient world and well into medieval times, and with good reason. It has its own antibacterial and antifungal properties, it is locally available to rich and poor alike in most parts of the world, and, of course, it tastes good. Later cooks would discover that honey takes a back seat to sugar when it comes to achieving the transparency, the bright colour and the pleasing gel of what we would now call jam. However, it would be many centuries before sugar would take its place on the world stage.

Sugar cane is native to Southeast Asia, and was first cultivated as a crop in New Guinea and Indonesia. It gradually spread to various other parts of Asia, and by the mid-sixth century BC it was being commercially grown in India, where it was noticed in 510 by the soldiers of Darius I of Persia. It had been introduced into southern China by 286 BC, but production did not really start to expand into the rest of the country until the sixth and seventh centuries AD. The Greeks certainly knew of sugar by 327 BC, because Alexander the Great's general Nearchos mentioned seeing it on a trip through India. However, even well into the first century AD, the Greeks thought of it strictly as a medicinal plant.

If one nation might be suggested as the inventor of jam and marmalade, Sasanian Persia, which was cultivating sugar by the sixth century AD, makes a good candidate. Besides sugar, Persian cooks had most of the classic jam fruits at their disposal very early on. Citron, quince and apples are likely native to Persia and were possibly first cultivated there. Bitter oranges may first have grown wild in Persia before being introduced to China and hybridized there to produce sweet oranges, and then returning to Persia with Portuguese traders. Cookbook author Najmieh Batmanglij points out that the sweet orange, 'ironically, took its Western name from the Persian *narenj*, or bitter orange, while in Iran, the sweet orange is called *porteqal*, after the Portuguese merchants who imported it.'[1]

Persian jam (known as *moraba* or *murabba*) differs from the Western idea of jam in that it consists of solid fruit pieces in syrup rather than semi-dissolved fruit in a gel. It is cherished as part of a classic Persian breakfast, *sobhaneh*, which includes such widely familiar elements as tea, milk, bread, butter, cheese, eggs, fruit, honey and some kind of preserve, often made from tree fruits like quince, apple, pomegranate, plum, cherry or citrus, rather than berries.

We have some evidence for the long history of quince and apple preserves from a Pahlavi text entitled *King Husrav and His Boy*.[2] King Husrav II of Persia, a historical figure who reigned AD 590–628, is also a character of literary legend. In this tale, a noble youth named Vasphur requests to be examined for admission into the king's service. The king asks him questions to test his nobility – not, as one might expect, having to do with his fighting prowess, learning or virtue, but instead about his knowledge of luxurious living. In what becomes a catalogue of sixth-century Persian fine dining, Husrav questions Vasphur about the best and most desirable meats, fruits, grains and wines (as well as music, flowers, women and horses). The fifth question is 'Which pastry is the finest and the best?' Vasphur answers, 'In summer: the almond-pastry, and the walnut-pastry, and the walnut-bun, and the bun made with fat, and the finger-pastry . . . that they fry in walnut-butter. But with the fruit-jelly that is squeezed out and filtered from the juice of the apple and the quince, no pastry can stand the contest!' In other words, by the sixth century AD, Persian nobility already thought of quince and apple preserves as the best of all desserts.

Clear evidence for the cooking of bitter-orange preserves in Persia by about 1300 can also be seen in these lines from the poet Bos-hac of Shiraz: 'Do not be grieved, O Sour Orange! Like the sweet orange, turn into preserves / And then your sourness will change into sweetness.'[3]

Persia may have been quick off the mark in developing its sugar-production capacities, but through the seventh century Baghdad also became an important producer, and sugar soon spread to the Mediterranean coast and beyond, spurring a huge enthusiasm for sweetmeats and sweetened drinks (considered to be healthful as well as delicious) through the Byzantine period.

Aam murabba (green mango jam).

Honey was still employed for preserving as well. *Kitab al-Ṭabīḫ* (The Book of Dishes), by the tenth-century Baghdadi writer Abu Muhammad al-Muthaffar ibn Nasr ibn Sayyār al-Warrāq, is considered to be the first-known Arabic cookbook. Among its six hundred recipes, it lists instructions for *tarbīb al-safarjal* (a preserve made by boiling quince in honey); honey-preserved fruits, known as *anbijāt*, which could be used as food or medicine; a rose-petal conserve called *jalanjabīn*; and recipes for preserving myrobalan (also known as cherry plum), citron, apples, pears, carrots, dates and ginger. They call for heady mixtures of such aromatic spices as cassia, black pepper, cloves, cardamom, mace, spikenard, nutmeg and saffron.[4]

Sugar's sculptural qualities fascinated chefs and their rich patrons, spurring all sorts of culinary experiments. 'A Persian visitor claimed that in 1040, the sultan's bakers transformed 162,000 pounds of sugar into a life-sized tree and other sweet replicas,' notes sugar historian Elizabeth Abbott.[5] All sorts of sugared fruits, fruit cheeses and fruits in syrup, precursors to our modern jams and marmalades, were created.

From 1095 to 1291 the taste for sugar arrived in Europe with returning crusaders, driving a revolution in culinary tastes, writes historian Susan Pinkard in her *A Revolution in Taste: The Rise of French Cuisine* (2009):

> Between the tenth and thirteenth centuries, dishes featuring Persian ingredients and cooking techniques became popular with elites in many parts of the Arabic-Islamic Empire . . . [D]ishes very similar to these eventually became popular on the tables of the elites of Latin Europe and surely provided the inspiration for the sweet and aromatic style that became so fashionable in the late Middle Ages.[6]

This watercolour of *c.* 1890 by Chinese artist Zhou Pei Qun shows a confectioner selling sweets to a small boy.

Meanwhile sugar cultivation, and with it the knowledge of sugar-preserved fruits, was known far beyond the Mediterranean. In China, the presence of Arab and Persian residents had already created an increased demand for sugar in the eighth century, and by the late Song dynasty (the twelfth and thirteenth centuries) all sorts of candied fruits and fruits in sugar syrups were extremely popular. They were sold by vendors at the night markets of Hangzhou and Kaifeng, served at tea-houses and stored in fancy porcelain jars to be given as gifts by the wealthy. Even today, street vendors in China offer candied fruits.

Marco Polo briefly mentioned sugar production in China, India and East Africa in 1285. Christopher Columbus planted sugar cane in the New World, a move that would supply sugar more cheaply to the world, at a cost of great human suffering brought about by the slave trade. Madeira, the Canary and Cape Verde Islands, São Tomé and West Africa were also sugar-producing regions by the fifteenth century.

However, as the Middle Ages came to an end, sugar was still largely a luxury of the rich, Europeans were not eating jam for breakfast, and fruit preserves did not yet have a consistency suitable for spreading on toast; in other words, jams and marmalades had not yet become their modern incarnations.

3
Elaborate Banqueting Dishes: The 1500s

The Renaissance saw a surge in world sugar production. The resulting drop in price spurred an extravagant enthusiasm for sugar creations of all sorts, especially in Italy, where sugar had already begun to replace honey around 1300. Food historian Peter Macinnis, author of *Bittersweet: The Story of Sugar*, estimates that the cost of sugar in Europe fell steadily from the equivalent of about u.s.$24 per kg in 1350–1400 to $6 in 1500–1550. In 1633 the English physician and author James Hart wrote, 'Sugar hath now succeeded honie, and is become of farre higher esteem.'[1] Over the next fifty years, the price would drop by half again.

Countries like Spain and Portugal began preserving their fruits in sugar for export to northern countries, especially quinces and, later, oranges. Some of these sweet Mediterranean exports, 'signalled by the suffix *-ade* . . . arrived in England already in boxes and pots. Among them were . . . citrinade, "gingerbrade", that is, gingerbread (made with green ginger and white ginger), pomade (made with apples) and succade'.[2] Hardy fruits like damsons, cherries and apricots were locally grown and preserved in northern Europe, and by the mid-sixteenth century, Mediterranean-style recipes for preserving fruit in sugar were appearing in such cookbooks as *The*

Secretes of the Reverende Maister Alexis of Piedmont, translated into English in 1558, and *A Book of Cookrye*, first published in London in 1584.

In Tudor England, although sugar was still out of reach for the poor, anyone with aspirations to the upper classes would present a range of fancy sweetmeats at the end of a formal dinner. One category of sweetmeats was the array of candied, or sugar-preserved, fruit, either dry or in syrup, known as 'suckets' (from 'succades'). These were made by macerating the fruit (letting it sit in sugar), and then heating it repeatedly, with resting periods in between, to allow the water content of the fruit to be replaced by sugar crystals. They were eventually stored in covered 'gallipots' (small earthenware jars).

Eating suckets properly – especially the sticky, wet ones – required the use of a special implement. The sucket spoon was a tool of the Tudor table; it had a spoon at one end for the syrup and a two-pronged fork at the other. They were also called sucket forks.

Solid fruit pastes were also in vogue. At first these were made only from quinces, which thicken easily; they gradually evolved into what we would now call marmalade, as well as the quince cheese called *membrillo* (among other names) that is prized anywhere in which Spanish or Portuguese is spoken.

German silver sucket fork of *c.* 1500.

The food writer C. Anne Wilson, in *The Book of Marmalade*, has deftly documented these transitions from the earliest-known version, a solid quince paste concocted by Greek physicians in the first century AD to treat digestive issues. It was simply made by sealing quince chunks in a pot with honey until they had partly dissolved.

The Greek name for this food, *melomeli* (apple honey), became Latin *melomeli* or *melimela*, which in turn led to the Portuguese word *marmelo*, meaning simply 'quince'. The Portuguese used the name *marmelada* for the solid tangy orange confection they manufactured and exported from quinces boiled down with sugar, from which English speakers derive the English word 'marmalade'.

Seasoned with flavourings like musk, pepper or rose water, this luxury product was produced in two versions: a thick jelly made from filtered quince juice, and a more solid type made with the pulp as well. They might be stamped with fancy designs like flowers, stars or crowns before being packed

The modern incarnation of the tangy quince cheese known as *membrillo*.

into wooden boxes, to be sliced and savoured at leisure. The word 'marmalade' – also rendered in variations like 'marmalett' – gradually evolved into a generic term for any fruit cheese. Sixteenth- and seventeenth-century cookbooks offer recipes for 'marmalades' of pears, apples, damsons, plums, cherries and so on.

The preserve made from the juice alone was called *cidonitum* in Latin, a name derived from the Greek term for quinces, *mēlon kudónion*, which means 'Cydonian apples'. This word was somewhat modified as it travelled through the various Romance languages of Europe: in England it became 'quiddony', while in France it became first *condoignac* and later *cotignac*. There, it is said, a chef from the town that is actually named Cotignac travelled to Orléans sometime in the Middle Ages with the recipe, which was enthusiastically received in his new home.

Legends have sprung up around this Cotignac d'Orléans, which is still made today from quince juice thickened with sugar and tinted with red food colouring. Joan of Arc was supposed to have been rewarded with it for some for her exploits in 1429, and it was apparently a favourite of more than one French king. Today it is considered to be an artisanal culinary treasure. Cotignac d'Orléans has been internationally recognized by the Ark of Taste, a project of the Slow Food Foundation for Biodiversity, which identifies traditional food products considered to be at risk of extinction. It is made by just one manufacturer, and only 25,000 precious little wooden boxes are filled per year to supply the entire world demand. Joan of Arc's picture is still on the label.

During the Renaissance, suckets and the various types of marmalades fell into the category of 'banqueting stuff' – what would now be called a sweet dessert course. When the host could afford it, the banquet was an extremely elaborate affair

France's traditional Cotignac d'Orléans, a quince cheese made since the Middle Ages.

that might be laid out in a separate room from the main dining room or even in a separate building, like a garden pavilion. In 1615 Gervase Markham's *The English Hus-wife* used the term 'banqueting dishes' in this way:

> Thus having showed you how to preserve, conserve, candy and make pastes of all kinds, in which four heads consists the whole art of banqueting dishes, I will now proceed to the ordering or setting forth of a banquet, wherein you shall observe that marchpanes have the first place, the middle place, and last place; your preserved fruits shall be dished up first, your pastes next, your wet suckets after them, then your dry suckets, then your marmalades and goodinyakes, then your comfits of all kinds, next, your pears, apples, wardens baked, raw or roasted, and your oranges and lemons sliced, and lastly your wafer cakes.

This wood and silver English sucket fork dates from the 1840s, but they were common implements at the Renaissance banquet table.

Such a 'banquet' would have been a dazzling procession of sugar-preserved fruits and nuts. Markham's 'marchpanes' (a word related to 'marzipan') are shaped biscuits made of crushed almonds and sugar. 'Goodinyake' is the same word as *cotignac* and 'pastes' can be made of almost any fruit. Markham says that these dishes are not frequently used, but points out rather damningly that 'whosoever is ignorant therein is lame, and but the half part of a complete housewife.'

4
Sweet Confections to End the Meal: The 1600s

European enthusiasm for fancy confectionary did not dim at all in the seventeenth century. Sugar was reaching Europe in increasing quantities from the New World and the taste for sweets was growing – particularly in England, as noted by historian Peter Macinnis: 'Between 1662 and 1775, English consumption of sugar increased twentyfold, and almost all of it came from the Americas.'[1] Sugar was still believed to be somewhat healthy, and, strange as it may seem to the modern reader, a centuries-old idea persisted that raw fruit was dangerous to eat, but that fruit cooked in sugar was a tonic.

By contrast, in China, although sugar production had grown enormously, its consumption never rose as dramatically as in Europe (and later in North America); maltose rather than sucrose became the sweetener of choice. Nonetheless, economic historian Sucheta Mazumdar points out that while Brazil was supplying almost the entire European demand in the 1630s with an output of about 45 million lb (more than 20 million kg) annually, China was exporting a very respectable 10–15 million lb (4.5–7 million kg). Most of this production was carried out by relatively small independent landowners, and even into the nineteenth century China did not have the slave-run plantations that arose in the Americas.

Juan van der Hamen, *Still-life with Sweets and Pottery*, 1627, oil on canvas, shows a variety of sugar confections, including candied whole fruits, jars of preserved fruits and the round wooden boxes used to contain quince or other fruit cheeses.

Sweet fruit preserves were enjoyed not just in sugar-mad England, but all over Europe. The still-life paintings of artists like Juan van der Hamen (1596–1631) and Georg Flegel (1566–1638) show that similar candied fruits, bottled preserves and fruit pastes were commonly being consumed by the upper middle classes in Spain, Germany and Austria within their lifetimes. In Italy, the Baroque cookbook *The Modern Steward* (1692–4) by Antonio Latini provided recipes for preserving fruit in syrup, and a formal dinner always finished with candied fruits and other confections.

In France this period saw a sharp growth in interest in cooking of all kinds. As early as 1555 Nostradamus – who is these days better known for his prognostications than for his culinary expertise – had published around thirty recipes for *confiture* in a collection of household recipes modestly titled *Excellent et moult utile opuscule* (Excellent and Most Useful Little

Work). (The French word *confiture* can be used to mean either a fruit paste or a jam-like preserve.) François la Varenne, author of an influential general cookbook of 1655 called *Le Cuisinier François*, also published *Le Confiturier François*, a complete guide to making preserves, syrups, cordials and similar confections, in 1661.

In some areas, prized regional specialities were already being made. For instance, in the town of Bar-le-Duc, generations of locals were being indoctrinated into the painstaking process that produces a world-famous redcurrant jam. Records going back to at least 1344 show that it was valued as a noble gift in the Middle Ages, and Renaissance royals like Mary, Queen of Scots are said to have sought it out. A 1916 article describes the unique process, which is still carried on today:

> During the month of July each year trained workers [known as the *épépineuses*, or seeders] receive from the factories quantities of currants, which they take home for the purpose of removing the seeds. In this process the berry is

This oil painting of about 1618 by Frans Snyders of a Brussels fruit market shows the wide variety of fresh produce available in northern Europe at the time.

Georg Flegel, *Still-life with Parrot*, *c.* 1620, oil on copper, shows an array of after-dinner sweets, including fresh and dried fruits, sugar confections and a wooden box of quince cheese (also known as *cotignac* or *membrillo*).

held in the fingers of one hand and the seeds are removed by means of a goose-quill sharpened to a fine point. The work is exceedingly difficult, and requires considerable dexterity acquired by long practice . . . The quantity of sugar used is much greater than in ordinary jams and jellies, owing to the fact that the jelly boils for only a short time in order to avoid the oversoftening of the berries.[2]

Bar-le-Duc jam.

In the mid- to late 1600s the extensive orchard at Louis XIV's palace at Versailles furnished a wide variety of preserves to be served at the end of the meal. By 1740 Jean Anthelme Brillat-Savarin (author of *La Physiologie du goût*) assumes that even a middle-class dinner for ten people would finish with a third course of cheese, fruit and a pot of preserves. In wealthy French households of the seventeenth century, writes culinary historian Florent Quellier,

> The noble fruits like pears, peaches and figs were especially prized, particularly if they came from the garden . . . [T]he word 'dessert' began to be replaced by 'fruit' among people of quality, and the principle function of the head of the orchards in the house of a king or a great lord was to supply fresh fruit, *confitures* [preserves] and *confiseries* [sweetmeats] for desserts and collations . . . Cooked with cane sugar or more rarely honey, fruits were eaten equally as compote, marmalade, syrup, jelly made from fruit juice, fruit paste – that is, dry preserves like the celebrated Cotignac d'Orléans – and in fruit confits.

In Scotland, likewise, wealthy families grew their own fruit to preserve alongside a steady supply of imported oranges and lemons. A notebook of 1683 from Dunrobin Castle, the seat of the earls of Sutherland, is full of sugar-rich recipes for fruit syrups, jellies, pastes and marmalades made from apples, quinces, cherries, raspberries, oranges, lemons, gooseberries and plums. But instead of being the domain of servants, points out food historian Olive Geddes, 'the tasks of collecting fruit and preserving it to provide delicacies and sweetmeats for the cold winter months ahead fell largely to gently-born women.'[3]

It was through this period that European cooks began to find a middle ground between the old-fashioned paste-like 'marmalades' and the preserves that consisted of whole or sliced fruit potted in syrup. For instance, some marmalade-makers began to experiment with chopping the orange rind into strips or 'chips' instead of crushing it into a paste. They also began to add apples to the mixture to give it a more gel-like (rather than syrupy) consistency.

In fact, orange peels are rich in pectin, so marmalade doesn't need apples to achieve a nice jelly. However, many of the older recipes called for the oranges to be soaked in several changes of water to reduce their bitterness, so much of that useful pectin would literally have been thrown out with the bathwater. Culinary historian C. Anne Wilson in *The Book of Marmalade* (first published in 1985) gives home cook Rebecca Price credit for being the first to write down a modern-style orange marmalade recipe using sliced peel and employing only the orange pith to achieve a gel, in 1681. Price also deserves bonus points, as it seems she was the first person ever to use the word 'jam' in print. (Its derivation, incidentally, has never been identified; the spelling 'giam' is sometimes used in early recipes.)

5

Elegant Desserts and Breakfast Preserves: The 1700s

It would be fair to say that no other nation has embraced jams, jellies and marmalades with the same vigour as Britain. The Georgian era (from the early 1700s to the beginning of the Victorian period in the 1830s) saw a number of connected developments that brought about a change from the early 1700s, when sweet preserves were still mainly served by the rich as after-dinner treats, to the later 1800s, when jam and bread became critical staples for the poor.

'One area in which eighteenth-century English cooks led the world was in finding new ways to use sugar,' remarks food historian Susan Pinkard, noting that the English population was consuming an average of 8 kg (18 lb) of sugar per person per year by the early 1800s, about 25 times what they had been eating at the beginning of the 1700s.[1] This was much more than the rest of Europe and other parts of the world; by way of comparison, Americans were only consuming about 2.8 kg (6.3 lb) per year in 1822.[2]

In the 1720s the sweet course began to be called 'dessert' in England rather than the 'banqueting' course. Fruit cheeses and candied fruits continued to be made. Some, like candied orange peel and cherries, were incorporated into new baked goods as well as into traditional dishes like mince pies and Christmas puddings. Few home cooks would think of making their own candied peel for Christmas baking these days, but in the 1700s, although such sweetmeats could be bought from a growing coterie of professional confectioners, many housewives and cooks in service to families preferred to make their own.

Sugar was becoming continuously more affordable through this period, as New World plantations, with their shameful reliance on slavery-based production, thrived. But there were other important developments. For one, the eighteenth century saw changes in daily eating patterns. In the 1600s wealthy Britons might have eaten cold meats for breakfast, while the poor were likely to start the day with a porridge of grains or legumes, and people of any means might have washed down their morning meal with ale, milk or a sweet drink. Through

Scones with jam and clotted cream: a teatime staple.

the 1700s English breakfast tables increasingly featured tea with bread and butter.

In Scotland, where it had been customary to begin the day with a shot of whisky in the 1600s, a radical shift occurred in the early 1700s when the practice of drinking tea and eating marmalade gained precedence instead. (This explains why classic recipes for Scottish-style marmalade often include a fair lacing of whisky.)

Tea had made its way to England for the first time in the 1660s, and tea-drinking was made fashionable partly through the influence of the Portuguese princess Catherine of Braganza, who married England's King Charles ii in 1662. It joined coffee, which had arrived in the 1630s, and chocolate, which came a bit later, as a stylish beverage to be consumed in public coffee houses and in wealthy homes. Over the next two centuries tea-drinking would trickle down (so to speak) to the less affluent, and caffeinated beverages with sugar replaced their alcoholic counterpart as the morning pick-me-up.

Throughout the UK, other meals also shifted into a fresh arrangement, presenting new opportunities for jam consumption at odd times of the day, as tea-focused meals were gradually inserted into the routine. By the mid-nineteenth century, the well-to-do gathered for light fare over afternoon tea, while those of lesser means indulged in a more substantial meal at 'high tea', eaten after the working day was over. In the 1850s, when the construction of the railroads brought tourists into the western counties Dorset, Devon and Cornwall, entrepreneurs popularized the idea of the indulgent 'cream tea'. Dollops of locally made strawberry jam and thick cream piled on inexpensive scones promised a good profit margin for those willing to dish it up with tea to pleasure-seeking Londoners.

Another sweetened fruit treat took on a new prominence among Georgian dessert foods. Jellies, common since medieval times, were now often being served in tall, elegant single-serving glasses instead of on a plate. These could be grouped in towers, perhaps arranged on an epergne (an ornamental holder) designed to show them off beautifully.

Before the advent of electric light, one of the ways wealthy Georgian hosts could impress their guests was by splurging on costly beeswax candles and arrangements of mirrors to illuminate their gatherings after dark. No doubt the translucent qualities of colourful jellies arranged in sparkling glasses on shining trays contributed to the desired effect of luminosity. As culinary historian Elizabeth David writes,

> How ravishing those eighteenth-century tables must have looked when the crystallised fruit, the oranges and raisins, the spun sugar confections, the trays of sylla-bubs, the pyramids of jellies, the dishes of little almond cakes shaped into knots and rings and bows, the march-panes spiked with candied fruit, the curd tarts and all the sweetmeats were spread.[3]

There are many different ways to get jelly to gel. When one thinks of jelly along with jam and marmalade, one might picture a jar of clear preserves thickened with the pectin found naturally in the fruit. But these sorts of jellies have a fairly soft set, and there is a long and rather grand tradition of fancy moulded jellies, which, to keep their shapes, must be set with animal protein derived from horns or hooves, or with vegetable starches like rice, sago, tapioca, carrageenan or agar-agar.

Historic-jelly expert Peter Brears traces the earliest-written jelly recipes to the fourteenth century, when cooks would

This dessert table, decorated with elaborate sugar sculptures, was laid out at a celebration for eighty people on 19 January 1746 in The Hague. Engraving from Juan de la Mata, *Arte de repostería* (1747).

reduce fish or pork in boiling water to produce a solid jelly with bits of meat or fish embedded in it, along the lines of the costly terrines that can still be bought in the better butcher shops. Over time, the adventurous spirit of generations of cooks produced innumerable creative variations, including ambitious sculptural arrangements moulded in the forms of towers, domes and shells, or cunningly made to resemble other types of food.

By Georgian times the preference was for sweet rather than meat-based recipes. Besides single-serving jellies in pretty glasses, the repertoire would have included intricate moulded jellies cunningly made into complicated shapes, forming a school of fish in a pond, for example, or a bird's nest full of eggs. In fact, because they were so often moulded into fancy forms, in mid-nineteenth to twentieth-century England, jelly desserts could be called simply 'shapes'.

Recreation of an 18th-century dessert table, complete with ornate moulded sugar embellishments, created by renowned food historian Ivan Day for the Gardiner Museum, Toronto, Canada.

An 1805 edition of *The Art of Cookery Made Plain and Easy* by the formidable Hannah Glasse (originally published in 1747) lists jellies, flummeries and syllabubs thickened with hartshorn (a powder made by grating the horns of a deer), isinglass (a fish product) or calves' feet, which all produce a sturdy gelatine. These are intended to be poured into individual cups, and are generally flavoured with lemon or orange and sugar. ('Most people love them sweet; and indeed they are good for nothing unless they are,' Glasse counsels.) Some of her recipes are strongly decorative, like the Ribband Jelly, set in layers of various colours, and the particularly entrancing 'Moon-shine', which consists of an almond blancmange embellished with an inset moon and stars made of clear lemon jelly.

Along with these is a recipe for currant jelly that is clearly meant to be not only served as a dessert, but stored for future use. Set with just the natural fruit pectin, it calls for only part of the jelly to be set in glasses; the rest is poured into gallipots; then brandy-soaked paper rounds are set over its surface, and more paper with holes pricked into it is tied over the top of the jars. A similar method, using rum instead of brandy, appears in Leo Tolstoy's *Anna Karenina*, which was published in the 1870s. Glycerine or egg whites could be employed for the same purpose.

Mya Sangster, a culinary researcher and historic cook at Fort York National Historic Site in Toronto, Canada, has experimented with several methods of preserving jams and jellies employed before the introduction of modern commercial jam jars. If they didn't tie papers over the preserves, cooks of past centuries might seal them with rendered animal fat to keep them airtight and insect-free. This is similar to the still-used practice of pouring melted paraffin over jam. Like the

Jam-filled 'Cake Sandwiches' from Mrs Dalgairns's *The Practice of Cookery* (1830), made at a workshop led by Mya Sangster at Fort York National Historic Site in Toronto.

paper method, they both work to a degree, but if the fat or paraffin pulls away from the side of the jar, the seal is compromised and the contents may spoil.

A third method is to tie pigs' bladders over the tops of the jars. Sangster found this somewhat effective, but rather time-consuming, as the bladders must be cleaned and worked by hand for some time to make them pliable enough to give a good seal.

Both gelatine- and pectin-thickened jellies certainly continued to be eaten right through to the present era, not only in England but in countries around the globe. Gelatine-based jelly desserts came within reach of every home cook with the proliferation of commercial jelly products: first, gelatine sheets that required soaking before use, and, later, convenient powder mixes.

The American Knox and Jell-O companies both started operation in the late nineteenth century, and from that time onwards North American households knew no shortage of home-prepared jelly dishes. These ranged from simple flavoured jelly in glass cups or bowls to ambitious, colourful moulded rings stuffed with decorative pieces of every imaginable food, from fruit sections to stuffed olives, ham cubes and hot-dog slices. Enthusiasm for these types of creations peaked in America in the 1950s and '60s, but has since fallen off, whereas pre-made jellies remain popular in Asia in the form of little plastic cups containing a single mouthful, in flavours ranging from apple and strawberry to lychee, guava and durian.

It must be said that there is something peculiar about jelly. It might seem innocuous – often used as a gentle food for invalids or children – but it also has a seamy side. This may be due to its quivering, wobbly texture, which seems to evoke the bouncier parts of the human body. (Think of Jack Lemmon in the movie *Some Like It Hot* (1959), remarking that Marilyn

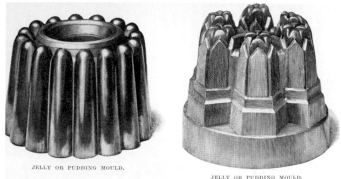

JELLY OR PUDDING MOULD.

JELLY OR PUDDING MOULD.

American household jelly or pudding moulds, from *Mrs Seely's Cook Book* (1902).

Monroe's departing posterior looks 'like Jell-O on springs', or the American pop song of the early twentieth century 'It Must Be Jelly ('Cause Jam Don't Shake Like That)'.

In the late nineteenth and early twentieth centuries jelly popped up in numerous scandalous associations, as in the nickname of musician Jelly Roll Morton, credited with composing the first jazz tune, 'Jelly Roll Blues', in 1910. This sort of jelly roll has nothing to do with baking and everything to do with sex. The metaphor was already present in Georgian times, when London saw a proliferation of 'jelly houses', where patrons could sit and order a glass of jelly to their table, like in a modern ice cream parlour.

The association may seem incongruous, but in the piazza at Covent Garden, jelly houses were known as places where prostitutes trawled for business as they sipped ratafia (an almond-flavoured brandy) and nibbled exotic jellies. Historian Dan Cruickshank reports the scandalized complaint of the Society for the Reformation of Manners in 1776 that the 'area's popular jelly-houses are now become the resort of abandoned Rakes and shameless Prostitutes', and that some

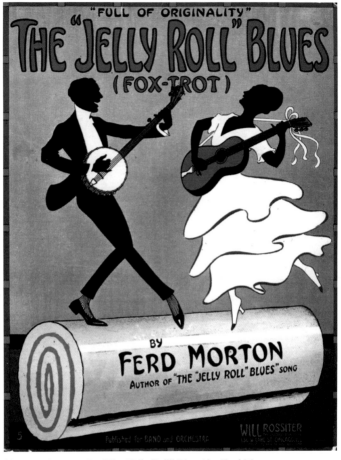

Sheet music cover for 'The "Jelly Roll" Blues' by Ferd Morton, 1915.

of these institutions 'offer an ample supply of Provisions for the flesh; while others abound for the consummation of the desires which are thus excited'.[4] A far cry, no doubt, from the intended use of Hannah Glasse's unexceptionable recipes.

6
Recipes for Home Cooks:
The 1800s

Through the seventeenth and eighteenth centuries, as sugar became ever cheaper, sweet preserves were increasingly seen as something that almost anyone might make at home or buy from a local purveyor (either a professional confectioner or a shopkeeper making small batches in season for local customers). The nineteenth century saw a great evolution of food-preserving techniques. The French cook Nicolas Appert (1749–1841) pioneered the modern method of preserving food in jars. He first presented his process, which entailed sealing food in airtight jars and subjecting it to high temperatures by boiling, in 1806. Then in 1810 he published his findings in a book titled *L'Art de conserver les substances animales et végétales* (The Art of Preserving Animal and Vegetable Substances).

Ceramic pots were still used to store preserves, but soon commercial manufacturers began to produce glass bottles for home cooks. In 1842 in the UK, Yorkshireman John Kilner started manufacturing a glass fruit jar with a screw-on lid that held a glass stopper in place. Kilner jars are still sold in the UK.

The U.S. saw a number of different approaches to the glass canning jar, beginning in 1858, when New Yorker John Landis Mason introduced his Mason jar, topped with a zinc lid and sealed with wax. (Later models used a glass lid and a rubber ring.) In 1882 Henry W. Putnam of Bennington, Vermont, invented the Lightning jar, with a glass lid held in place by a wire bail. Regardless of patents, numerous competitors emerged through the late 1800s.

Around 1898 five brothers from Buffalo, New York, noticed that the original Mason patent had expired and founded Ball Brothers Glass Manufacturing Company to produce Mason-style jars; they also acquired other brands, such as Alexander H. Kerr's Hermetic Fruit Jar Company, which introduced a jar sealed with a metal lid held in place with a screw-on metal band in 1915. This technology eventually superseded the others, and today Jarden Home Brands, a descendant of the Ball company, enjoys a virtual monopoly in North America, selling glass jars with two-part lids under the brand names Ball, Kerr and Golden Harvest in the u.s. and Bernardin in Canada.

As every level of society gained the means to make their own preserves – from windfall fruit, if necessary – a new class of recipes was developed or expanded: baking with jam. Recipes from authors like Hannah Glasse continued to circulate (with and without credit) throughout the nineteenth century, and simple treats like jam tarts and 'puffs' or turnovers became commonplace. As culinary historian Sidney Mintz writes, 'by instructing the rising middle classes in the fabrication of pastries and other desserts, Mrs Glasse provides rich documentation that sugar was no longer a medicine, a spice, or a plaything of the powerful.'[1]

Puddings became a standard vehicle for the use of jam and especially marmalade. The term 'pudding' in the nineteenth century covered a range of dishes, from steamed or boiled globes like the traditional Christmas pudding to much more exotic creations, and recipes ranged from the

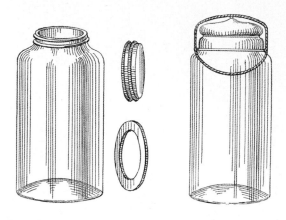

Fig. 86 Glass Jars for Canning, eith Metal top and Rubber

References : - A , Mason Jar, patent ; a , metal top ; b, rubber. B, "Lightning" patent jar

of canned rruit complete ; with adjustable wire fastening for saving breakage.

Illustration of canning jars by May Rivers from B. F. Hurst, *The Fruit Grower's Guide* (1905). Left: a screw-top jar with rubber ring; right: a bail-top closure.

thrifty to the spectacular – such as the impressive Nesselrode pudding. Said to have been created by the legendary French chef Carème (1784–1833), it is an extravaganza of chestnut ice cream stuffed with dried fruit, moulded into the shape of a boiled pudding and served with maraschino liqueur, a sweet, almond-like beverage made from Marasca cherries. By 1889 the Jewish-American *'Aunt Babette's' Cook Book* offered a variation of the Nesselrode pudding with apricot marmalade, candied cherries and preserved figs in place of the currants and raisins of earlier incarnations.

Homelier puddings abound. In 1827 Esther Copley, writing as 'A Lady', published *The New London Cookery and Complete Domestic Guide*, which contains one of many extant recipes for Portugal Pudding, a wholesome concoction of rice flour or

S 1. Jelly of two colours.   T 1. Raspberry Cream.   U 1. Centre Dish of various Fruits
    V 1. Trifle.   W 1. Strawberries au naturel in ornamental Flowerpot.

This illustration from Mrs Beeton's *Book of Household Management* (1861) shows a two-layer jelly (top left).

semolina baked with sugar and eggs and generally served with raspberry or apricot jam, or (as in Copley's recipe), with both. English writer Richard Dolby's *The Cook's Dictionary, and House-keeper's Directory* of 1830 includes an Apple Pudding with Pistachio Nuts, which calls for the apples and nuts to be stewed together with 'rather more than half a pot of apricot marma-lade', and then baked in pastry and served with yet more marmalade over the top. *The Lady's Receipt-book* of 1847 by the American cookbook author Eliza Leslie offers instructions for economical single-serving marmalade puddings made with stale biscuit crumbs, eggs and cream. Once baked, they are to be slit open and filled with 'any sort of nice marmalade or jam'.

Baltimore-based writer Elizabeth E. Lea's 1845 *Domestic Cookery* incorporates sweet preserves into other types of des-serts like Whips (a pretty parfait of whipped cream, beaten egg whites and apple jelly) and Floating Island. The latter, a French creation, is still well known. It consists of meringue 'islands' floating on a milk or custard 'lake'; Lea's variation calls for currant jelly to sweeten the meringue.

Mary Johnson Bailey Lincoln was the author of *Mrs Lincoln's Boston Cook Book: What to Do and What Not to Do in Cooking*, published in 1884, one of the publications that offers the recipe for the delightfully named Apple Porcupine, made with apples covered with meringue, spiked with almond 'quills' and baked. Mrs Lincoln advises to 'put quince jelly among the apples'. Twelve years later, Fannie Farmer's famous *Boston Cooking-school Cook Book* omits the meringue and the jelly bath, but suggests filling the apples with 'jelly, marmalade, or preserved fruit' before adding the almonds.

'Mrs Lincoln' is fairly creative with preserves; she suggests topping omelettes with jam or marmalade, and provides a recipe for sweet rice croquettes: breaded and fried rice balls like

Italian *arancini*, but filled with dried fruit, jelly or marmalade instead of a savoury stuffing. This is not the earliest version of such a recipe, however; as early as 1830, Richard Dolby published a very similar recipe for croquettes of rice stuffed with marmalade.

Regardless of their usefulness in cooking, certain preserves made from beloved local fruits have inspired particular affection in the hearts of various nations. For example, lingonberry preserves are particularly loved in the Scandinavian countries; plum jams are prized in Eastern Europe; Italians adore their aromatic bitter orange preserves; and Egyptians hold a special place in their hearts for the jam made from the little apricots they call *mishmish*. But in some locales, an extra level of associations and traditions has sprung up around the making and eating of fruit preserves.

The Welcoming Preserve: Spoon Sweets

As previously mentioned, the modern conception of jam as semi-dissolved fruit suspended in a fairly thick, spreadable jelly is relatively recent. In many traditions (like Persian cuisine), the most common sweet preserves resemble the older conception of whole pieces of fruit in a thick syrup. The beloved *glyko tou koutaliou*, or spoon sweets, of Greece and Cyprus fall into this category.

They are called spoon sweets because they are served in a particular way, as part of a little ritual to welcome guests into the home. Imagine arriving on a hot afternoon, tired, dehydrated and overheated, into the refreshing breezy shade of a Mediterranean home. How pleasant to be given a glass of cool water and a shot of strong coffee along with a fragrant spoonful of preserved cherries, bitter oranges or apricots, most likely served from a special glass dish! The Lonely Planet *World Food* guide to Greece describes this tradition as follows:

> The elaborate services of crystal or silver . . . attest to the aesthetic importance of the spoon sweet. In Constantinople there was an entire industry dedicated to their production . . . Usually they come in small bowls with demitasse spoons hanging from the edge. It is accompanied by a set of tiny saucers and delicate glass tumblers for water.[2]

This custom can be found in many countries, but is especially prevalent in Greece and Cyprus, where its precise origins are lost. In their earliest versions, the fruits would have been preserved in honey or *petimezi* (grape molasses, something like

Sour cherry spoon sweets.

the Roman *defrutum*). By the Byzantine period sugar was becoming the preservative of choice – although some present-day recipes still call for the older ingredients.

It is not only fruits that are used in *glyko*, but nuts, flowers and some surprising foods like aubergine and pumpkin. In her short history of spoon sweets, the Greek cookbook author Diane Kochilas points out that different items are traditionally preserved as they come into season, and that various regions of Greece have particular specialities: lemon and orange blossom in Andros; grape, fig and mandarin in Chios; and 'in Santorini and Kos, small tomatoes seasoned with cinnamon and studded with blanched almonds are preserved in syrup'.[3] Strawberries, quince, apples, pears, plums, oranges, bergamot, watermelon rind and pistachios are also used.

'The history of Greek spoon sweets has hardly been traced,' write Andrew Dalby and Rachel Dalby in their book *Gifts of the Gods: A History of Food in Greece* (2017).[4] However, they note, mentions pop up from time to time in food records over several centuries. The American banker and financier Nicholas Biddle may be the first English writer to have noted the welcoming custom in 1806, when he wrote that 'On entering a house you are first presented with a pipe, then coffee, and sometimes a spoon full of citron and a bowl of water.' However, as early as the tenth century, there are mentions of *glyko* in *De Ceremoniis*, the 'book of ceremonies' of the Byzantine emperor Constantine VII Porphyrogennetos. When the English clergyman and author George Wheler travelled to the city of Chalcis in Euboea in 1682, he saw a variety of spoon sweets, but thought 'they would hardly please some of our nice [English] ladies'.[5]

Around this time Chios was already a notable source of spoon sweets, and the records of one fancy ambassadorial banquet there state that 'four little cupids were continually serving spoon sweets, fruits and drinks to the ladies.' Perhaps these ladies, being resident in Greece, did appreciate them. Certainly Isabel J. Armstrong, author of *Two Roving English-women in Greece* (1893), enjoyed her first taste – presented in glass jars along with water and coffee – very much. She wrote that 'The light coloured jam that we tasted was something like pear marmalade and strongly to be recommended.'[6]

In any case, spoon sweets remain dear to the hearts of Greek citizens and expatriates. Though they can be purchased, they are meant to be made in the home. Canadian sisters Helen and Billie of the food blog 'Mia Kouppa' recall fondly their childhood exposure to the sticky treats: 'Every Greek family we knew, including ours, seemed to have jars and jars of sweet, syrupy dessert ready and waiting; perfect for unexpected guests, and for satisfying a craving for something sweet.' Many years later, as adults, they asked their parents to make quince spoon sweets for them, 'and a few hours later they pulled out a little glass plate and offered us some to taste. We knew that this recipe was perfect, because as our spoon hit the glass, and the quince touched our lips, we were children again.'[7]

Varenye: The Preserve of Last Resort

Generally speaking, in countries where fruit is plentiful and winters are short or non-existent, sweet preserves are valued for their intense flavours. In places known for their harsh, barren winters, where February starvation has been a distinct possibility as recently as the early twentieth century, however, they have come to mean a lot more.

In Russia, for example, *varenye* is a beloved national tradition. One gets a sense of the importance of *varenye* to the Russian psyche in discovering that in 2015, to celebrate Russia's

Georgian peach *varenye*.

Strawberry *varenye* from Azerbaijan.

Year of Literature, the Voronezh branch of the Russian government newspaper *Rossiyskaya Gazeta* held a festival called Literary Varenye. Over the summer, participants made *varenye* from recipes associated with great Russian literary figures at museums in former estates around the country.

From a culinary point of view, *varenye* is more or less interchangeable with Greek spoon sweets or the preserves known as *murabba* in Persia, the Caucasus and parts of South Asia: not really a jam, but a preserve of fairly solid fruit pieces in a thick syrup. Part of the knack of cooking it is to know exactly how much heat the fruit can take before it begins to break down. It's a tricky skill that takes practice to acquire, and is therefore associated with wifely maturity.

In the novel *Anna Karenina* (1877), the young Kitty Shcherbatsky locks horns with the trusted and very experienced housekeeper Agafya Mikhailovna over the cooking of strawberry *varenye*. Kitty maintains that it can be done without adding water; the older woman is angry about her presumption, and hopes the batch will be spoiled so that she will be proven right. She is disappointed, however, and thus Kitty takes a step towards establishing herself as a woman to be taken seriously.

As is traditional, the ladies of *Anna Karenina* make their preserves outdoors in the countryside, on a charcoal brazier. This is significant, because true *varenye* is supposed to be made not with produce purchased from the grocer, but with precious foraged fruits and berries: wild strawberries, bilberries, blueberries, whortleberries, raspberries, blackberries, cloudberries, lingonberries or cranberries.[8]

Varenye is loved as a topping for pancakes and as a filling for little pies or the dumplings known as *vareniki*. However, it is valued not only for its uses as a condiment, but as a bulwark against winter food shortages, and it was traditionally a

This 1876 oil painting by Vladimir Makovsky is titled Варят варенье (Making Varenye). It shows a Russian couple making *varenye* in the traditional way.

housewife's duty to maintain a good supply. This sentiment was embraced by Russian Jews, who understood the precariousness of life. As Benjamin Shinewald wrote in an essay in the *Winnipeg Free Press*,

> If their homes were burned down, at least they had a jar or two of varenye to tide them over until they could rebuild . . . as late as the 1970s, Israeli Prime Minister Golda Meir half-jokingly referred to Israel's nuclear arsenal as its varenye. Just as these fruit preserves gave pre-Holocaust Jews some measure of comfort in the face of danger, Israel's nuclear arms would give the same measure of comfort to post-Holocaust Jews. Varenye remained, barely, a synonym for a bit of security in a wildly insecure world.[9]

7
Ventures in Commercial Marmalade

With the dawn of the Industrial Revolution, a new kind of preserve-maker appeared in Britain: the large-scale commercial producer. And once again, Scotland led the way. For marmalade fans, Janet Keiller (1737–1813) is a figure of mythic status, virtually credited with creating marmalade single-handedly. Of course marmalade in various forms had existed long before Keiller, the wife of a Scottish merchant, famously preserved a shipwrecked cargo of Seville oranges so that they could be sold before spoiling. She can, however, fairly be credited with popularizing the technique of slicing the orange peel into 'chips' instead of mashing it into a paste, which was already done in Scotland but was not yet the dominant method.

More significantly, she and her family became early prototypes of modern commercial food enterprise as their business grew from a modest family concern into a multinational brand. No one is certain when Janet Keiller began making marmalade, but a factory opened in 1797 under the name of James Keiller. As W. M. Mathew, who has written extensively about the firm, points out, 'In the course of their development they grew from a small grocery establishment in the centre of Dundee to a company which, in 1914, owned three factory complexes, in Dundee, London and Tangermünde in Germany, and more than two dozen overseas branches and depots as far afield as Toronto, Buenos Aires, Cape Town, Sydney, Shanghai, and Yokohama.'[1] In 1857, renamed James Keiller & Son, the company turned clearly towards the model of a modern manufacturer when it set out to avoid Britain's heavy sugar duty by locating production facilities offshore – literally – on the island of Guernsey. The Guernsey plant operated until 1879, by which time the sugar duty had been abolished. Keiller then opened a factory at London's Tay Wharf.

As early as 1867 more than 3,000 chests of bitter oranges were arriving every year from Seville, creating four hundred jobs in the city. Keiller used about 1.5 million jars each year from the Maling pottery works at Newcastle upon Tyne. Originally white-glazed earthenware and later made from glass, the jars were a marker of quality, and were proudly blazoned with the honours and prizes awarded to Keiller over the years.

After five generations of Keillers, control moved into the hands of another family, the Boyds, who had worked as managers for the company. Keiller continued to thrive, winning the contract to supply preserves to British troops during the First World War. Keiller almost doubled its profits annually during the war, despite heavy competition and the wartime shortages of sugar, fruit and male workers.

But profits fell off in peacetime, and in 1919 Keiller was sold to Crosse & Blackwell. ('The Boyds, displaying only weak loyalty to the Keiller name, seem to have cashed in their recently acquired majority holding with minimal compunction,' Mathew tartly points out.)[2] Keiller passed in subsequent decades through a succession of very large food corporations – among them Nestlé, Barker & Dobson, Cadbury and, most recently, Hain Celestial. It may surprise some who grew up thinking of the Keiller name as an iconic brand to realize how far it has moved from being a family business or even

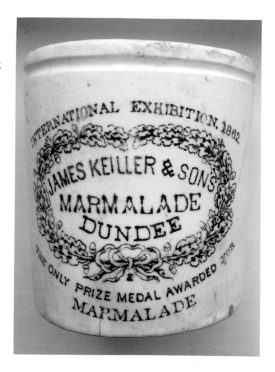

Keiller's marmalade jar of the 1860s from the Maling Pottery works.

a dominant player. These days, its legacy is perhaps best perpetuated in the glazed jars with their quaintly elegant oak-leaf wreath that still serve as pen-holders in the homes of so many marmalade aficionados.

Moir's Daring Gambit

Another early pioneer, John Moir & Son, attempted a coup in the late 1870s that – had it worked – could have established the company as Britain's most important marmalade maker. In 1822 John Moir pioneered the commercial production of tinned foods in Aberdeen. In 1877 the firm somehow managed to convince the Spanish king Alfonso XII to grant it an exclusive licence to pulp Seville oranges for export. The following year it moved its head office to London and launched a shot across the bows of Britain's other commercial marmalade makers in the form of an advertising campaign promoting the freshness and goodness of the oranges to be 'delivered daily, fresh gathered from the gardens' to its Spanish factory, and comparing the oranges with great disparagement to the inferior product that all the other makers were content to use.

John Moir & Son branded its product as 'Seville Orange Marmalade' and took steps to prevent other companies from using that name, which it actually registered as a trademark. But the tide of business was too strong to be turned, and competitors were so insistent in breaching the trademark that after about 1880, John Moir & Son gave up its bid to corner the Seville marmalade market.

By that time the company had passed its peak; it was saved from total extinction almost by chance. In 1920 John Moir & Son had opened a production facility in Cape Town. Over the next few decades, British operations limped along, but these were eventually liquidated in 1950; however, the brand took hold in South Africa, and Moir's baking ingredients and dessert mixes are still popular there.

Thus, though John Moir & Son is no longer remembered in Britain, it leaves a significant legacy, noted by the University of Warwick's Kirsty Hooper, who seems to be the sole scholar to have appreciated the significance of John Moir & Son's brief blaze of marmalade glory. 'While the term "Seville Orange Marmalade" had been used occasionally by other manufacturers during the 19th century, it seems never to have stuck,' she points out. 'Moir & Son brought the term into popular usage, restoring the Iberian dimension of "Scotch" marmalade after three centuries of progressive Scotticization.'[3]

More Marmalade Mavens: Robertson, Rose and Cooper

Other, later, marmalade specialists carved out distinctive niches and unique markets for themselves. For instance, legend says that Marion McFadyen of Paisley, Scotland, first began to make marmalade under her husband James Robertson's name in 1864 because the soft-hearted grocer kept buying unsaleable bitter oranges from a local vendor. Robertson's Golden Shred soon caught on with the public, and the business grew steadily.

In 1910 James Robertson's son John had the idea of adopting a 'Golly' doll as its brand mascot. The golly, or golliwog, once popular as a toy, is now considered to be a racist caricature of a minstrel show performer with African features, including black skin and woolly hair, wearing a blue tailcoat, yellow vest and red trousers. However, in the early twentieth century, British consumers were so fond of the mascot that Robertson's went a step further, creating a loyalty programme that allowed children who collected tokens printed on or tucked underneath the jar labels to post them in to collect premiums. Thus was born an immensely popular series of collectible enamel pins showing Golly in every conceivable occupation and outfit, beginning with a golly golfer in 1928.

After embracing the campaign for about fifty years, the British public finally started to object to it. Nonetheless, Golly endured for a further fifteen years. The last pin was created for an exhibit about Robertson's in Paisley in 2000, and Golly was discontinued altogether in 2001; by that time, more than 20 million pins had been distributed, and avid collectors still treasure them. Robertson's Golden Shred survives today, but with the inoffensive marmalade-loving Paddington Bear on the label.

Pre-First World
War Robertson's
marmalade
golly pin.

In 1867 the Merchant Shipping Act required British ships
to carry lime juice as a protection against scurvy, which was
a stroke of luck for Leith merchant Lauchlan Rose, who had
just patented a process to preserve fresh lime juice without
alcohol, thus winning the hearts of Temperance advocates
and the Royal Navy (which was still relying on lime juice to
protect its sailors from scurvy) in a single leap. He moved to
London in 1875 to produce his now-famous Rose's Lime Juice
Cordial. By the early twentieth century, L. Rose & Co. had
become one of the most important sources of industry for
the island of Dominica, making it the world's leading lime
producer. However, it wasn't until the 1930s that the firm
began to produce its lime marmalade, marketed with the
slogan 'The Difference is Delightful'. It was a hit with the
public. Today the company's offices have disappeared from
London, and the limes are imported from Africa, but you
can still buy Rose's Lime, Lemon, or Lemon and Lime 'fine
cut marmalade' in attractive faceted and embossed glass jars.

In 1874 Sarah Jane Cooper (née Gill), wife of Oxford shop-keeper Frank Cooper, manufactured the first batch of 'Frank Cooper's' marmalade, using her mother's recipe. (Her accomplishment is still celebrated with a street plaque in Oxford.) She retired in 1899, but a grand Frank Cooper's factory opened in Oxford in 1901. Because Cooper's marmalade was served at the University of Oxford, it grew especially dear to alumni, who carried it to all parts of the world.

Frank Cooper's 1903 marmalade factory, Frideswide Square, Oxford, now repurposed as 'The Jam Factory'.

Recently, in the course of documenting and conserving the Terra Nova Hut – a shelter used by South Pole explorer Robert Scott (1868–1912) – the Antarctic Heritage Trust of New Zealand found an unopened tin of Frank Cooper's Oxford Marmalade. The trust was able to unwrap and restore the paper label that still covered the corroded can, but the contents were inedible. Frank Cooper was taken over by Brown & Polson in 1964 and eventually acquired by the Hain Daniels Group in 2012 with Hartley's, as well as Robertson's and Rose's, uniting all four competitors within one gigantic corporation.

8
A Great Jam-factory Explosion: Victorian Entrepreneurs

Today, Crosse & Blackwell is associated with well-loved products like Major Grey's Chutney. In 1868, however, it was said to supply one-quarter of the jam and marmalade in London and this represented 25 per cent of their total output of sweet spreads. Their main export markets were in India, Australia and China.[1] They also operated factories in the u.s., Canada, South Africa, Argentina and France.

The company was founded by two school friends, Edmund Crosse and Thomas Blackwell, who were apprenticed together in 1819 to a pickle- and sauce-making firm called West & Wyatt in London's Soho district. By 1830 they had risen so high in the business that they were able to buy it from their former master, William Wyatt, upon his retirement, and open under the new name of Crosse & Blackwell.

From the beginning, the two partners seem to have understood how food manufacturing would change over the next century, and by the mid-1800s they were employing business practices far ahead of their time. They had a keen nose for brands and marketing, and managed to develop, buy or represent some of the world's best-known condiments, like Lea & Perrins Worcestershire Sauce, Branston Pickle and, as we have seen, Keiller's Dundee Orange Marmalade.

Also noteworthy was their approach to their supply chain. Instead of seeing themselves solely as a condiment-making company, they made sure they could control as many of their important supplies as possible, with a vinegar brewery for pickle production, an in-house tin department and glass factory to manufacture food containers and wharf properties to facilitate shipping.

They were canny in understanding food trends and fashions, importing recipes and ingredients from the colonies to make the highly spiced curries and chutneys that pleased the Victorian palate. They also brought the celebrity chefs of the day, like Charles Elmé Francatelli, a former chef to Queen Victoria, into their own kitchens to oversee production, according to urban archaeologists Nigel Jeffries, Lyn Blackmore and David Sorapure, who co-authored an archaeological report on the business.[2]

When jams and marmalades were first introduced in 1840, they represented only a small part of Crosse & Blackwell's product lines. But in the early 1870s, when Britain's high duty on sugar was reduced, and then dropped altogether, jam suddenly became affordable for low-income consumers – cheaper than butter – and 'bread and jam became the chief food of poor children for two meals out of three'.[3] Crosse & Blackwell were well placed to take advantage of the market's enormous growth, and their sweet spreads became a more prominent segment of their product lines.

In 2010, after London's Crossrail Ltd announced plans to redevelop part of the Tottenham Court Road Underground Station, the Museum of London Archaeology (MOLA) unit explored the site, which had been the location of Crosse & Blackwell's London factories between 1830 and 1921. Excavators uncovered a treasure trove of jars and bottles in good condition: 13,000 pieces, the largest collection of pottery ever unearthed on a London site. Much of the collection was made up of containers for the Household Jam, Jams and Jellies (especially raspberry, redcurrant and plum) and Pure Orange Marmalade lines.

Today some Crosse & Blackwell preserves are still sold, but the brand was acquired by Nestlé in 1960 and taken over by the American J. M. Smucker Company in 2004. The name still conjures up an image of good, carefully made food, as it has for almost two hundred years.

The trickle of commercial producers that had begun in the early 1800s turned to a flood by the end of the century. In the 1870s, when England's sugar duty was abolished, numerous companies moved their offices and production facilities into London, where convenient transportation by water and rail meant they no longer needed to be situated near the orchards that produced their fruit, and goods could easily be shipped across the globe.

Sugar prices dropped and demand grew, until by 1906 'there were 200–300 jam-makers [in Britain], the five largest between them using 20,000 tons of fruit a year.'[4] As the cheaper product caught on with the poorer classes, a distinction arose between producers of what was thought of as 'preserves' (which denoted a more prestigious product, although, confusingly, it was still employed as a generic term for any fruit preserved in sugar) and everyday 'jam', the food of the masses. E. & T. Pink, once an immensely successful company, would fall into the latter category.

Pink's: Low Wages and Cheap Jam

Pink's was founded in 1860 by grocer Edward Pink. By 1874 it was employing more than four hundred people in a

Bermondsey factory as the jam market broadened with the falling price of sugar. Bottling cheap jam for the working class, Pink's would bring in as many as two hundred extra workers during the busy seasons. By 1879 Edward Pink & Sons claimed to be the largest manufacturer of preserves in the market.

Among other cost-saving measures, Pink's added glucose to their jam, and pushed workers particularly hard, even by the standards of rough-and-tumble Bermondsey, the district of London south of the Thames where food factories were clustering, partly because of its convenient access to the river, and partly because it was not subject to the same regulations that governed businesses in the city centre.

When Edward Pink's son Thomas renamed the business 'E. & T. Pink', around 1890, it employed some 2,000 workers, but by the early 1900s it was facing hard times due to the postwar economic collapse and a costly fire in 1918, as well as increasing labour unrest from factory workers who chafed under harsh conditions and poor wages. During Bermondsey's 1911 strike by women factory workers, to be discussed in more detail further on, 'At the Pink's factory, which was known locally as the Bastille, girls carried banners inscribed with the slogan "We are not white slaves, but Pink's slaves".'[5] By 1920 the meteoric rise was fizzling out, and Pink's was taken over by a competitor. The E. & T. Pink name, tarnished by its many reverses, was allowed to die out, and the enormous Bermondsey factory complex was demolished in 1935.

It is tempting to imagine that the fate of Pink's, rising so high and being cast so low within a single generation, was an act of karma. The huge success of the business was built on the principles of grinding workers at low wages to produce the cheapest possible product for consumers who could afford nothing better. There are other ways to run a jam factory, as is well demonstrated by the stories of the rural factories like Hartley's, Chivers and Wilkin.

Hartley's: The Benevolent Capitalist

William Hartley was a pioneer among a group of rural jam-makers whose factories were as inviting and whose workers as well treated as could be imagined in late Victorian Britain. Raised in a Primitive Methodist family, he seems to have absorbed the very best of the 'Christian' values of selflessness and diligence. He started out as a grocer in Pendle, Lancashire, and drifted by chance towards the manufacture of preserves in 1871.

Although Hartley's did not grow much of its own fruit, it secured a supply of the best produce available, and processed it quickly, using the works of many hands, in season. Hartley's refused to use substandard fruits or preservatives, and only switched from fresh, whole fruits to pulp reluctantly in 1941, under the duress of the Second World War. 'The season for soft fruits started . . . in June when the first strawberries were gathered . . . followed by the arrival of French and then English blackcurrants, red currants . . . gooseberries, raspberries, plums, damsons and finally blackberries, the last of which were picked in early October,' writes descendant and historian Nicholas Hartley.[6]

Hartley's workers enjoyed unusually high labour standards, with profit-sharing, a pension fund and a benevolent fund that were continued long after his death. In 1886 William Hartley & Sons Ltd moved to Aintree, Liverpool, and built a model village for its workers. In 1911, Hartley built the Hartley Homes, twenty almshouses whose maintenance he provided for in perpetuity. His factory used early examples of ergonomic workplace design; for instance, some of the women stood in small pits so they would not strain their backs by bending to handle the produce.

In 1890 Hartley's appointed a u.s. agent, and its products were soon available in grocery stores and railway dining cars across North America. In 1901 the company built a 0.8-hectare (2 ac) factory in London, christened Green Walk. It was equipped with electricity, the most modern fire sprinklers and equipment capable of turning out 4,000 tonnes of jam every month in peak season. It was spared the worst of the bombings in the Second World War and continued in operation until 1975.

Hartley died, well-loved, in 1922, and his descendants ran the business with care for several decades, but wartime rationing was a blow, and by 1959 the family was ready to surrender the business to the soft-drink giant Schweppes, which also acquired Chivers and Sons, Rose's and Moorhouse (which had been founded out of a grocery business in 1881, initially to make 'lemon cheese', a thick fruit paste). Still, the brand continued to be popular, and Hartley's jams and jellies are still widely available as part of the Hain Daniels Group, based in Leeds.

Chivers: The Orchard Factory

Another illustrious rural factory was Chivers & Sons, which for more than 75 years thrived in an idyllic countryside setting near the villages of Histon and Impington, just north of Cambridge. Although it grew to a prodigious size, with operating equipment that could fill as many as 80,000 tins per day, like Hartley's, Chivers maintained a wholesome rural character that allowed it to keep the quality of its products high while providing pleasant working conditions for its employees.

Even at its largest, Chivers's farm and orchards were employing what would now be called biodynamic practices, such as allowing their pigs and chickens to roam in the orchards and feed on leftovers from the fruit canning process, which in return provided both fertilizer and pesticide-free insect control. The blossoming fruit trees were much admired, and Rosemary Kovacs, a volunteer historic cook at Fort York National Historic Site in Toronto, Canada, who grew up in the Impington area, has told the author in conversation how residents of the area used to love the orchards and the factory smells: strawberry in spring and orange in winter.

The farm business was started by Stephen Chivers in 1806; his sons William and John would transport produce by road to their depot at Bradford, about 290 km (180 mi.) away, where they noticed that much of the fruit was being bought up by jam-makers. They soon decided that they should capitalize on their own produce, and it was John's son Stephen who made the first batch of jam in a converted barn in 1873. He eventually took over the whole operation and expanded jam production, adding marmalade made with imported oranges in 1889 so the workers and equipment would have something to do through the winter.

The Chivers enterprise was a leader in mechanizing its production processes, developing its own canning machinery before any other business in Europe. In its heyday the company was also fabricating its own boxes, cans, barrels and baskets, and the factory site had a sawmill, a blacksmith and a carriage works. In 1900 it was the largest of Britain's farm-based preserve companies. It weathered the downturn after the First World War well, and by 1921, when some of the other Victorian jam businesses were beginning to falter, it was employing 2,000 to 3,000 workers, depending on the season, and producing as much as 20,000 tonnes of jam per year.

Like Hartley's, Chivers & Sons was infused with an upright Protestant sense of morality. Since so much of the jam production – even the fruit sorting – was done by machinery, most of the workers were involved in farming and fruit picking, or in ancillary functions like carpentry. Chivers had a pension scheme by 1895, and supported the growth of a workers' community that by 1897 was served by its own doctor and fire brigade. A souvenir brochure produced by the company in the early 1920s describes the life of the local worker as one of virtuous pastoral serenity:

> The bulk of the workers live in Histon or the other villages round, and hundreds of them come to the factory upon their bicycles. Others travel in from Cambridge, a special train and fleet of buses being arranged morning and evening for their benefit. Great care is exercised in the selection of these workers and their health and welfare are looked after by a staff of trained nurses. Adjoining the factory premises, stands an old country residence which now serves as an institute for the women and its beautiful grounds are open for their use during meal times and in the summer evenings.

From the 'Orchard Factory', thousands of jars and tins of preserves were pouring to every corner of the globe. The company's Olde English Thick Cut Marmalade, soon nicknamed 'The Aristocrat of the Breakfast Table', was introduced in 1907. (It is still available under the Hartley's brand.) The company opened a raspberry cannery in Montrose, Scotland, in 1925 and a factory in Dublin, Ireland, in 1932. By 1938, at the height of its powers, Chivers & Sons was the largest fruit and vegetable canning company in England, employing around 4,500 people.

Still operating as a family business, Chivers added two more factories through the 1940s, but by the end of the Second World War the company that had led the world in mechanical production was being left behind by others that were taking advantage of newer, more efficient technology. In 1959 Chivers & Sons joined Hartley's as part of Schweppes. In 2004 the brand disappeared, except in Ireland, leaving behind only sweet memories for many of its aficionados.

Wilkin & Sons of Tiptree

Like Chivers and Hartley's, Wilkin & Sons started as a fruit farm. Throughout its history it has demonstrated an abiding respect for the fresh fruit and berries lovingly raised in rich soil that was in the nineteenth century nurtured by applications of lime, mussels and starfish; manure from the streets of London; and guano from Peru. Maura Benham, author of *The Story of Tiptree Jam: The First Hundred Years, 1885–1985* (1985), writes that founder Arthur Charles Wilkin didn't begin to make jam until 1883, when he was 48 years old. The idea came to him one day when he was carrying home some jam he had purchased and realized he might as well save himself both trouble and money by making it himself.

At first the jams were little more than a sideline – the farm was the steady earner – but Wilkin went a step further in 1885, when he created the Britannia Fruit Preserving Company with two partners. It didn't take long for people to start demanding the Tiptree brand for their breakfast tables; in 1905 the name was changed to Wilkin & Sons, Ltd, to differentiate the brand from other firms using the word 'Britannia'.

The first batches of jam were cooked up in the farm kitchen, using just six preserving pans that ran night and day in peak fruit seasons. At the suggestion of a merchant from Australia, Wilkin decided to call his product 'conserves' (rather than jam or preserves), because the word seemed to carry connotations of quality and value. The company lived up to those standards; even when production volumes grew, much of the fruit was processed within a few hours of picking. For about one hundred years a unique Wilkin speciality has been the strawberry jam made with the Little Scarlet berry (*Fragaria virginiana*), a tiny, flavourful variety bred by the Wilkins to offer the taste and texture of a wild berry. No other farm grows them; when the jam is available, it sells internationally for about u.s.\$14 or £11 per 340-gram (12 oz) jar.

Wilkin & Sons was especially rigorous about maintaining the purity of its ingredients at a time when food adulteration was rife. Common practices in the late Victorian period included substituting corn syrup for sugar, adding artificial flavourings and toxic coal-tar colourings, and using fruit pulp or cheap produce like apples in place of whatever choicer ingredients might be listed on the label. (After the turn of the century, suffragette Emmeline Pankhurst apparently started

Main entrance to the Wilkin & Sons factory in Tiptree, Essex, England.

her own jam factory with fair working conditions, in outrage at discovering an entire industry of women who were hired to carve wood into tiny counterfeit raspberry pips!)

In contrast, during the Second World War, when fresh Seville oranges were not available in great enough quantities to keep up with marmalade production, rather than offering poorer-quality products under the usual label, Wilkin & Sons created a new wartime brand name so consumers wouldn't be misled or disappointed by the diminished quality. As late as the 1950s the company still had little cold storage space, and most jams were made from fresh fruit.

Like Hartley's and Chivers, Wilkin & Sons always supported the welfare of its workers and maintained a reputation for exploring innovations in technology without sacrificing the virtues of its traditional production methods. Sometimes, it pays to insist on high standards: after four generations and almost 135 years, the Wilkin family is still involved in the management of this proud and excellent brand.

Most of the British jam, jelly and marmalade concerns that were founded in the nineteenth century have now disappeared or been absorbed into other companies. There are exceptions like Wilkin, or Duerr's, a fifth-generation fruit-preserve business that has leapt from strength to strength since it was founded in 1881 by Mancunian Fred Duerr. (In 2006 the company celebrated its 125th birthday by issuing a special jar of marmalade made with Pol Roger vintage champagne, Dalmore 62 whisky and pure gold leaf. Billed as the world's most expensive marmalade and valued at more than £5,000, it was auctioned on eBay for charity.) But for most jam- and marmalade-makers, the twentieth century would be a time of transformation, in terms of economics, technology and labour standards.

9
The Workers Boil Over: Labour Unrest in Edwardian London

As jam and marmalade factories proliferated through the late nineteenth and early twentieth centuries – especially in England and Scotland – the workers who made and bottled the products faced a bittersweet situation. On the positive side, preserve-making offered a whole new employment sector. Some jam factories operated seasonally, overworking employees during the short summer-fruit season and leaving them without employment for long stretches of the year. But others could operate year-round by making marmalade in the winter, jam in the summer and other types of foods such as chutneys or sauces in between. These companies were a boon for the lowest-paid workers, who were most susceptible to being laid off.

Between 1890 and 1914 in Glasgow, for instance, workers 'benefited from the emergence of integrated jam, preserve and pickle-producing factories which effectively ironed out the worst excesses of seasonality of production', writes researcher J. H. Treble. Opportunity for employment mushroomed there in the early twentieth century. Whereas the class of 'Jam, preserve, sweetmakers' was not even mentioned in the 1891

Census, by 1901 there were 146 men and 1,278 women listed as working in this category; ten years later, the numbers had risen to 455 men and 1,841 women, who together represented 1.83 per cent of the city's total workforce.[1]

The high number of female workers was not unusual. 'Throughout the nineteenth century much continued to be done by hand, for instance the sorting and grading of fruit'; vats were also stirred by hand, and workers often did not even use thermometers to judge when the preserves would set.[2] Because the work required such homely kitchen skills, it was considered a natural employment for women. However, as the English social reformer Helen Bosanquet pointed out in her forward-looking 1902 article 'A Study of Women's Wages', the general supposition of the times that married women needed less money than their single counterparts – or that women in general had less need of a steady wage than men – set up a double standard that has never quite been eradicated, even today.

But the increase in factory jobs was a double-edged sword for the poorest Britons. As women went to work, many of the time-consuming daily food-preparation duties, which had helped them feed their families on a shoestring in the past, fell by the wayside. Instead of baking their own bread, they were buying cheap baked goods that were frequently adulterated with chalk and other unpalatable additives to stretch the flour further. In fact, in late Victorian England, white bread, cheap jam (also commonly adulterated) and sweet tea became the filling but nutrient-poor staples of low-income women and children, with meat tending to be reserved only for the working men, and fresh fruit or vegetables being in short supply for all.

Nonetheless, low-skilled women were so eager for employment in the jam- and marmalade-making factories that they would take this dangerous and exhausting work for low pay, even though plenty of better-paid, less-harsh jobs were available. One explanation, Bosanquet suggested, was that many women were partly dependent on various types of charity relief, which would be cut off if they found better-paid work. Thus, she wrote,

> Any adventurous jam-maker can be sure, by settling in London, of getting as many female workers as he likes for about 7 [shillings] a week – certainly not a subsistence wage in London; and having got them he may treat them pretty much as he likes. He may turn them off for weeks or months in slack times; they will be there as soon as he chooses to open his doors again. He may work them day and night in busy seasons until they are broken down with fatigue and sleeplessness; and they will agree with the law which says it is all right. He may work them under conditions fatal to health, and they will take it as all in the day's work. The one thing which will never happen is that he should be 'short of hands'.[3]

Christina Black, a pioneering activist for women's and labour rights, interviewed nineteen women working as jam-makers, preserve-makers and mineral-water workers for her 1915 study *Married Women's Work*. For ten or eleven shillings per week, they carried out exhausting tasks, with some routinely lifting up to 25 kg (56 lb). 'It is difficult to believe that the carrying or piling up of pans or trays weighing half a hundred-weight each can be suitable for women who are expecting the birth of a child,' Black remarks drily – and in fact one mother of four 'grubby but healthy' children expressed her fear that three others had died 'quite young' due 'to her working right up to her time'.

Black describes another woman whose job involved pre-paring vegetables in a jam and pickle factory as 'aged 35, but looks worn and old' – and no wonder. While working for eight shillings a week (of which three went to rent just three rooms), she was keeping her home 'fairly clean and tidy' and caring for three children and a husband recuperating from a back injury sustained at his job on the docks. (Workers could pay as much as eight shillings a week in rent. Black mentions one woman who was paying this sum for just two rooms that housed three adults and two children.)

There were deaths in the jam factories. In 1893 fifteen-year-old Delilah Figgins died of septicaemia after a bruise on her leg became infected; her parents blamed the filthy con-ditions at the Pink's factory in Bermondsey, where she had been hired only ten days earlier. In 1895 another Pink's worker, Eliza Wrightly, was scalded to death when she fell into a pan of boiling apples. In 1900 even the reputable Keiller lost an employee named Rosalie Reed, who died after apparently slip-ping off a walkway into a 7-metre (23 ft) hole where boiling water was released; her body was not found until the day after she went missing.[4]

These dreadful working conditions were not universal. Photos and contemporary accounts demonstrate that some factories, like Wilkin and Hartley's, were pleasant environ-ments where workers were well looked after. Food historian Peter J. Atkins makes the point that those companies that ori-ginated on fruit farms in the countryside tended to be decent places to work, whereas the urban grocery businesses that used the poorest ingredients to grind out the highest-possible profits saw little reason to treat their workers well, knowing they had a limitless supply of cheap labour.

These were grimmer employers, and among these – although it was a huge and profitable enterprise – Pink's seems to have been particularly hard on its employees. In 1892 sixty of Pink's approximately four hundred women workers went on strike to protest a pay cut. However, their action had little effect, because so many other women were clamouring to replace them. That year 'the activist Clement Edwards urged the Co-operative societies to boycott Pink's products' for their intimidation tactics, and in the following few years legal and political pressure forced the company to allow workers to leave the workplace during their breaks, and to build a separate employees' dining room.[5] These moves were no doubt spurred on by the spectre of Delilah Figgins, whose parents had connected her death in the previous year to her being forced to eat her lunch amid half-rotten fruit.

It was not until August 1911 that the simmering anger of London's women jam-makers would come to the boil. Ursula de la Mare tells the fascinating story of the uprising of 15,000 women workers in Bermondsey, the neighbourhood along the south bank of the Thames where food factories tended to cluster. It was a time of rebellion; in that same year, London's male dockworkers were on strike, the suffragettes were active, and even schoolchildren across Britain staged strikes against long hours and beatings. Across the Atlantic, public revulsion against the conditions that had killed 146 sweatshop workers (123 women and 23 men) in New York City's Triangle Shirtwaist factory fire of 25 March would bring about permanent and sweeping changes to American labour laws as well.

Although British textile workers were mainly unionized by that time, food workers were not. The 1911 strikes broke out in the midst of a stifling heat wave, as women factory workers spontaneously decided they would not tolerate brutal conditions any longer. As George Dangerfield wrote 25 years later,

Pink's factory workers marching in the streets of Bermondsey for better wages and working conditions, 1911.

The story of the Bermondsey women seems almost to have isolated – with its mingling elements of unreason and necessity and gaiety and rage – the various spirits of the whole Unrest. One stifling August morning . . . the women workers in a large confectionery factory . . . in the 'black patch' of London, suddenly left work. As they went through the streets, shouting and singing, other women left their factories and workshops and came pouring out to join them . . . Very soon the streets were filled with women, and fetid with the smells of jam, glue, pickles and flesh. It was then, when they were all out, that the women discovered what they had come out for. Their average wages were 7s. to 9s a week for women and 3s. for girls: they wanted an increase.[6]

Over the next few chaotic days, the National Federation of Women Workers (NFWW) stepped in to help organize the workers and collect relief supplies of bread and milk. It was over quickly. At a victory rally held on 19 August,

'Fifteen thousand women, seething with rage and excitement, cheered [noted trade union leader] Ben Tillett in a meeting at Southwark Park.'[7] The strike ultimately brought about wage increases in nineteen of 22 factories, along with the creation of twenty new unions (though not all formally recognized by employers) and a permanent branch of the NFWW in Bermondsey, bolstered by 4,000 new recruits, according to historian Ursula de la Mare.

Dangerfield reports that 'The total gain was over £7,000 a year, in wage increases from one to four shillings a week.' At Pink's, wages rose from 9 to 11 shillings per week, but the battle was not yet over. In 1914 about 1,000 Pink's employees went on strike to demand further wage increases. 'Pink's response was to close the entire factory, citing safety concerns for those among his workforce who remained loyal. This left a total of 1,200 to 1,500 people idle. Work resumed after Pink agreed to grant the minimum wage recommended by the Trade Board.'[8]

Perhaps overall the rapid growth of Britain's commercial fruit-preserving industry was more of a gain than a loss for unskilled labourers. Certainly, thousands of new jobs were created. Women in particular now had a new way of earning money, and while many suffered at the hands of exploitive employers, as time passed, more companies offered decent working conditions and wages. Significantly, the jam factories drew women into the labour movement, where they discovered a new way to exercise their power in society.

10
International Condiment Empires

Britain may be the most jam-hungry nation, but fruit pre-serves are commercially produced all over the world. Australia lends a colourful chapter to the story with the history of its best-known national brand, IXL. The name, which at first glance resembles a Roman numeral, is in fact the motto of its irrepressible founder, Sir Henry Jones: 'I excel!'

Born in 1862 in Hobart Town, Jones went to work at the age of twelve, pasting labels onto tins in a jam factory. From this bottom rung, he rose up in the company until, upon the retirement of its owner, George Peacock, he took over. From his takeover in 1891, he operated the business as H. Jones & Co. Although he was nicknamed 'Jam Tin Jones', he was active in many business interests and was knighted in 1919, after which he became popularly referred to as the 'Knight of the Jam Tin'. His achievements have long survived him; the pre-serves are still being sold, and his Hobart warehouses, with some of the original equipment, are preserved as an upscale art hotel.

With its Commonwealth heritage, Australia was fertile ground for jam manufacturing. The same could be said of Canada, where grocery wholesaler Francis Adam Shirriff founded the Imperial Extract Company in Toronto in 1886 to formulate fruit flavour extracts, perfumes, essential oils and baking powders. In the early 1900s Imperial Extract added instant jelly powders, jams and marmalade to the product roster, to great success. By the 1960s, the company, renamed 'Shirriff's', was manufacturing in three countries, including Jamaica. It won the hearts of Canadians with a wildly popular promotion: colourful metal or plastic coins framing portraits of beloved ice-hockey stars, offered as premiums with the jelly powders and coveted to this day by avid collectors. Shirriff's was bought by Kellogg, the cereal company, in 1969. In 1988 its marmalade lines were sold to the American J. M. Smucker Company, while the jelly powders went to the Germany-based Dr Oetker. They are still sold under the Shirriff's brand name; the three-fruit Good Morning Marmalade was Canada's most popular orange marmalade as recently as the latest available survey in 2008.

Canadians were disappointed a few years ago when the long-established E. D. Smith was also sold to an American

Crates of Australia's IXL Jams being loaded for shipping, c. 1925–45.

Canadian jam and marmalade entrepreneur Francis Adam Shirriff, 1926.

firm, TreeHouse Foods Inc. Founded in the fertile Niagara area in 1878 by a noted fruit farmer and politician named Ernest D'Israeli Smith, it had remained in the family until 2002. The United States was not so quick to develop its own fruit-preserving companies. In the 1930s, notes Nicholas Hartley, a Hartley's salesman named Robert Delapenha reported that, although Crosse & Blackwell had already opened a u.s. factory, there was 'not a single brand of jams, jellies, marmalade or preserves being marketed nationally through the United States, nor is the consumer being told why she should eat jams, jellies, or marmalade.'[1]

One of the first distinctively American companies to emerge was Welch's, known above all for its grape jelly. It was founded by a former Wesleyan Methodist preacher named Dr

Tins of Canada's E. D. Smith jam.

Thomas Bramwell Welch, initially to provide a non-alcoholic grape drink to be used at communion services. Methodist historian Betty O'Brien writes that

> Using locally grown grapes and the techniques Louis Pasteur . . . had developed in the 1850s to control fermentation of wine, Welch experimented until he was able in 1869 to produce the first bottles of 'Dr Welch's Unfermented Wine.' He found preparing a non-alcoholic substitute for wine was relatively easy, but convincing churches to buy it was quite another matter.[2]

He persevered, however, and his non-alcoholic grape juice was adopted for shipboard fare by the u.s. Navy in 1913. The first jam, Grapelade, arrived in 1918 and was bought up by the u.s. Army. There it became popular with soldiers, who asked for it upon their return home. Welch's tangy and distinctive Concord grape jelly has become a standard filling for the classic peanut butter and jelly (or peanut butter and jam for British readers) sandwich. Andrew F. Smith's *Peanuts: The Illustrious History of the Goober Pea* (2002) finds that the earliest-known recipe was published in 1901, and that the combination was originally considered a ritzy treat. As the ingredients cheapened, it became a staple for American children during the Depression, just as jam and bread had sustained London's Victorian and Edwardian poor. Today Welch's continues as a co-operative of small family-run fruit farms, and Welch's preserves, juices, jelly powders and fruit-based snack foods enjoy undiminished popularity.

Also as American as apple pie is the J. M. Smucker Company. In fact, it was founded in 1897 by Jerome Monroe Smucker, an Ohio maker of apple cider (not necessarily of the alcoholic sort); he also sold apple butter from a horse-drawn cart as a sideline that eventually grew into a full-scale preserving company. The Smucker's brand associates itself

An American staple: the peanut butter and jelly (jam) sandwich.

with old-fashioned Americana, making the claim that J. M. Smucker's first apples grew on trees planted by the legendary Johnny Appleseed.

Smucker used to sign every cask of cider personally, and the glass jars of Smucker's preserves are still embossed with a facsimile of his autograph. The lids are printed with a red gingham pattern that mimics the look of a homemade preserve in a country kitchen. (This led to a 2011 copyright tussle with Andros, owners of the French brand Bonne Maman, which also distinguishes its products with a red gingham lid: what you might call a tempest in a jam jar.)

Today J. M. Smucker is far from a modest artisanal manufacturer. It has expanded to encompass dozens of other food companies in numerous categories. Its preserve brands alone include Double Fruit, Santa Cruz Organic, Knott's Berry Farm, Dickinson's and even the venerable Crosse & Blackwell.

Similarly, Hain Daniels Group, based in Leeds, England, now owns Hartley's, Robertson's, Rose's, Frank Cooper's and William's. But perhaps the world's largest fruit-preserve concern is Hero, a Swiss company that was founded in Lenzburg in 1886 as Henckell & Zeiler. It was originally named for its owners (a farmer and a jam-maker), but in 1920, after the death of Gustav Zeiler, it changed its name to Hero, which combines the first syllables of the last names of Gustav Henckell and his new partner Carl Roth.

The business thrived even during the Second World War, when its sugar-reduced line, Hero Delicia, was a hit with consumers. Hero diversified into various types of prepared foods and baby foods, and in 1995 it was briefly taken over by Schwartau International GmbH, part of the Oetker food empire. However, in 2002, Hero bought a majority share of Schwartau and began to purchase other international food brands, including established lines of preserves.

Today Hero produces and sells jams and jellies in numerous world markets, including its own brand of strawberry, raspberry, cherry, bitter orange, apricot, pineapple and fig jams. It cannily adapts its offerings to local tastes: for instance, under the Egypt-based Vitrac label, it can be found in Turkey and the Middle East as a purveyor of preserves that would have been familiar to the earliest Persian jam-makers, with flavours that include rose, bitter orange, fig and date. In Germany, its Schwartau jam and jelly lines include plum, cherry and forest berry, and in Brazil, the Queensberry brand has classic, 'wellness' and diet lines of fresh, tangy flavours like strawberry, tangerine, guava and blackberry. In Portugal, as Casa de Mateus, its offerings even include a quince 'marmalada' – sold in a little box that is not wood, of course, but plastic.

The models of Hero, Hain Daniels and Smucker's exemplify the trajectory of the twentieth century, which saw innumerable small family enterprises grow into national or international brands, only to slip out of the hands of their founders and into the balance sheets of enormous multinational corporations. But this is not quite the final chapter of the story of jams, jellies and marmalades.

II

Offerings from the Home Front: Wartime Preserving

In the dark wartime years of the twentieth century, the homely act of canning fruit united thousands of women to comfort and nurture the ill, the injured, the orphaned and the dispossessed by preserving millions of kilograms of fruit that might otherwise have gone to waste and shipping it over great distances to those in need. In the UK, the Women's Institutes carried the banner with their astonishingly prolific Fruit Preservation Scheme.

The Women's Institutes (WI) have for the past hundred years been powerhouses of rural community activity. They are especially known for preserving, a perception that has given rise to the gently teasing descriptor 'Jam and Jerusalem', which also refers to their common practice of singing hymns at meetings. Many Britons may not realize the WI were the brainchild of a Canadian, Adelaide Hoodless (1857–1910), who embarked on a crusade to educate women about domestic science after losing a child to tainted milk.

In 1896 a farmer named Erland Lee attended one of her public appearances. He was active in the provincial Farmers' Institutes, which existed to advance agricultural and livestock knowledge, and he was so impressed that he invited Hoodless to speak in 1897 before his local branch in Stoney Creek,

Let Your Fruit Trees Save Sugar

American propaganda poster by Robert Moore Brinkerhoff, *c.* 1917.

Ontario. It was at that meeting that Hoodless – possibly on the spur of the moment – suggested that there should be some parallel institution for women in rural communities that would provide the same sort of networking and knowledge-sharing in domestic matters that the Farmers' Institutes already did for farming concerns.

A few weeks later, 101 women turned up for a planning meeting, and the Canadian WI grew quickly. By 1909 there were

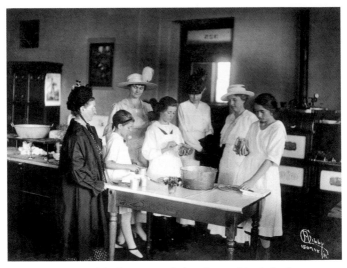

Children teaching adults how to can fruit and vegetables in Spokane, Washington, as part of an anti-waste campaign during the First World War.

36 chapters; by 1919, there were more than eight hundred. In 1915, after a Canadian WI member spread the word, the first meeting of the British WI was held in Llanfairpwllgwyngyll gogerychwyrndrobwllllantysiliogogogoch, Wales. The movement quickly took root in the UK, and it was already well enough established before the end of the First World War that members were able to import preserving equipment from the U.S., train women to can fruit on a large scale, commandeer supplies of rationed sugar and organize group canning sessions. It was during the Second World War, however, that they would see their finest hour.

Canning historian Sue Shepherd writes, 'The great plum glut of 1940 galvanised the national Federation of Women's Institutes into setting up Fruit Preserving Stations, run by women volunteers, across the country, in church halls, kitchens of stately homes, school canteens and empty warehouses.'[1]

'Can vegetables, fruit and the Kaiser too' poster: a piece of American propaganda from the First World War encouraging patriotic food preserving.

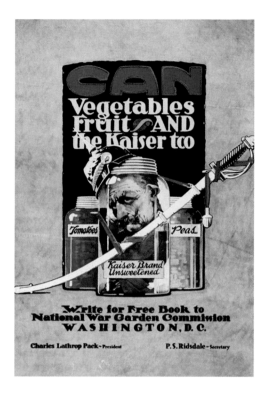

With sugar strictly rationed, they used substitutes whenever possible: glucose, honey, saccharine and sugar beet. Women's Institutes historian Charles Batey writes that

> The women of America sent 'Five hundred canners and a complete canning unit – a miniature canning factory . . . The Ministry of Food made over to the Institute movement the administration of the entire rural side of its war-time fruit-preserving programme . . . The Preservation Centres dealt only with fruit which could not be used by its growers nor transported to a jam factory, and so was in danger of going to waste. Non-members

Mrs Fidel Romero of New Mexico proudly exhibits her prodigious supply of home-canned food, 1946.

as well as Institute members were brought in to help in the task of jam-making, bottling and canning.[2]

The output was prodigious; in 1941 alone, Batey writes, 5,000 Preservation Centres churned out more than 2,000 tonnes of preserves and rescued 1,300 tonnes of fruit from spoiling. The volunteers were not allowed to buy the fruit of their labours; they worked to help the war effort. Indeed, they were: commercial producers were challenged by sugar rationing, and the factory conglomeration of Bermondsey was targeted by German bombers during the Blitz in a campaign to reduce Britain's food resources even further.

Back in Canada, the original Women's Institutes had not forgotten their British sisters. A past president of the Ontario Women's Institutes, Mildred Summers, writing in the *Canadian Red Cross Despatch*, tells how, at the beginning of the Second

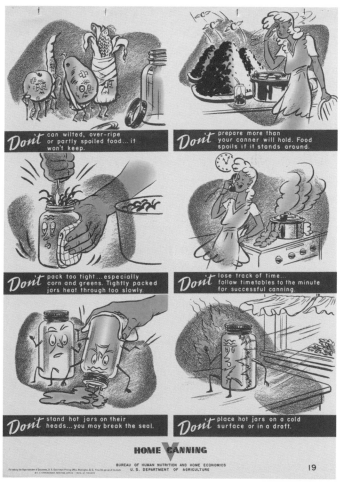

Safe canning instructions explained in a 1943 poster from the U.S. Department of Agriculture.

World War, a woman named Mrs T. B. Barrett (born Marjorie Clarke) stopped into the Women's Voluntary Service booth at Toronto's annual Canadian National Exhibition to ask about war work for rural women. Following a casual conversation with other visitors, she returned to her small town of Port Dover inspired to find a way to divert windfall fruit from her region's plentiful supply to some useful purpose. She enlisted the help of Sam Morris, editor of the local *Port Dover Maple Leaf* newspaper, who told her, 'Get everyone doing up jam in pint jars and I'll go to town on it in the *Maple Leaf.*' The excitement was infectious, Summers writes:

> With the energy and capability of these enthusiastic folk backing the Norfolk County Jam project, an unbeliev-able amount of jam was cooked by willing helpers. Even the summer visitors [to this lakeside holiday destination] stirred jam. The result was [that] 11,500 lbs. [5,200 kg] of jam put up in glass pint jars went to England and Scotland. That first year shipping the jam was a problem and the shipping charges for the greater part had to be paid by Norfolk County Women's Institutes. However, the Canadian Red Cross became interested in what these rural women were doing and the last shipment went under Red Cross auspices.[3]

The Canadian Red Cross Society's Annual Reports docu-ment the ensuing efforts, which soon became a national project. They record that in the spring of 1940, Canada's Red Cross passed a resolution to become formally involved, and appointed Colonel John A. Cooper to chair a jam-making sub-committee; he set a quota of around 90,000 kg (200,000 lb) of jam to be produced in just three provinces (Ontario, British Columbia and Quebec). With the Red Cross prepared

The Red Cross label was affixed to tins produced by Canadians in the Jam for Britain campaign. This one was returned to its source by a grateful recipient, a freed French POW who received raspberry jam aboard a British ship. (The postmark is barely visible on the reverse.)

to supply containers and shipping, the Women's Institutes were approached to contribute fruit, sugar and labour. (The food supplies were not drawn from personal stocks, but purchased through fundraising drives.) In 1940 the volunteer jam-makers canned 62,944 kg (138,768 lb) of jam, and 54,340 kg (119,800 lb) were shipped: more than ten times what the Norfolk pioneers had managed to produce the previous summer.

With their seemingly boundless energy and enthusiasm – as one must recall that these same women were simultaneously raising their own families and helping to run their own farms – members of the Canadian Women's Institutes pushed jam production well past what had initially been imagined. The tins provided by the Red Cross held 2.25 kg (5 lb) of jam each, and resembled gallon paint cans when filled, sealed and labelled. Photos of the period show proud groups of women posing with towering pyramids of processed cans, and parallel images of pink-cheeked British toddlers delightedly waving spoonsful of jam scooped out of brimming Red Cross tins.

In 1941 the whole country took part in what became known as 'Jam for Britain' (even though jelly, honey, maple syrup and maple sugar were added to the list of products being

Because Lorne and Emma (née Ainsworth) Brickman opened the doors of their factory one day per week to the Rednersville Women's Institute, located in Prince Edward County, Ontario, the branch was able to turn out 4,000 kg (8,800 lb) of jam during the Second World War, thought to be the most of any institute. Here, Lorne Brickman poses beside his truck, with crates of jam ready for shipment overseas.

shipped). Canadian women came just short of quadrupling the previous year's output, canning 208,919 kg (460,588 lb) of food. The project was repeated annually until 1945; the total wartime yield was 1,120,166 kg (2,469,545 lb) (not counting the first year's work in Port Dover).

Volunteers contributed whatever produce was most plentiful in their region, from tree fruits to wild berries. The project was taken so seriously that Canada's federal Sugar Administration supplied special allotments of sugar to the volunteers, and by the end of the war some canning was being handled by commercial producers. The wi raised so much money to support the project that they had enough leftover funds to purchase and ship concentrated orange juice, tomato juice and baby food to the uk.

The efforts poured into Jam for Britain were of real assistance to a nation that was feeling the pinch of hunger more every year. Beneficiaries included the sick and wounded in hospitals, children in war nurseries, servicemen and women and others assisted by the Women's Voluntary Services and the British Red Cross. One story recalls that

> the Lome [*sic*] Brickman factory in Ameliasburg township [Ontario] devoted one day a week to the production of jam which was donated to the Canadian Red Cross. Most of the jam was distributed overseas to organizations caring for British war orphans, but some of it found its way on board a British vessel evacuating French prisoners of war from Russia. After years of uncertainty and deprivation, the Frenchmen considered the jam a treasured gift symbolizing their freedom.[4]

As the lean war years wore on, who can imagine how much comfort would have come from the fresh flavour of a spoonful of lovingly made country jam on a bland slice of war loaf? Besides providing precious calories and some vitamins, wartime jam must have satisfied the craving for some literal sweetness in bitter times.

12

New Voices: Jams, Jellies and Marmalades in the Twenty-first Century

After the end of the Second World War, the thrifty spirit that had galvanized so many women during wartime gave way to a new peacetime fascination with convenience foods, and the women who had once canned fruits and vegetables every summer no longer felt compelled to do so if they could buy the tinned or frozen produce that was flooding the burgeoning supermarket chains of the 1950s. Those in rural areas continued to put up food in jars, but urban dwellers generally abandoned it for a time.

There were exceptions. The back-to-the-land movements of the 1960s and '70s saw a brief resurgence of culinary self-sufficiency, but that too died away in the affluent 1980s. Rising interest in fitness and diet regimes further tended to dampen demand for sweet foods, as it encouraged sales of sugar- and calorie-reduced spreads. However, jams, jellies and marmalades in their many incarnations have not ceased to be favourite foods around the world, as breakfast condiments and as ingredients in many types of recipes.

These days, sweet preserves are most frequently used in baking recipes – homemade or commercially produced – like

Sugar-free and reduced-sugar jams became popular in the 1980s.

'thumbprints' or 'bird's nest cookies': plain drop cookies embellished with a teaspoonful of jam in a central depression. These are known as *hallongrotta* (raspberry caves) in Sweden.

Numerous incarnations of a jam- or jelly-filled sandwich cookie have spread through Germany, Austria, the UK, the Scandinavian countries and North America. They often feature a round, star-shaped or heart-shaped hole in the upper crust to show off the filling, and it may surprise some Anglophiles that the classic commercial version, the 'Jammie Dodger', loved in Great Britain, was only introduced in the 1960s, and by a Canadian company – Weston's Bakery of Toronto – at that. Likewise, the pastry known as the 'Danish', a spiral of pastry topped with fruit, jam and/or nuts, actually originated in Austria. The Danish connection is supposed to have arisen during a bakery strike in 1850, when Danish employers hired Viennese bakers to keep production going.

The humble jelly doughnut is embraced by many nations. Originating in Germany, the jelly-filled, fried dough balls became *paczki* in Poland, *sonhos* in Portugal, Berliners (from their place of origin) in the U.S. and bismarcks (after the German

Jam-filled Czech Christmas cookies.

Thumbprint cookies are a popular way to use up leftover jam.

Jammie Dodgers, possibly the world's best-loved sandwich cookie.

chancellor) in parts of the United States and Canada. In Hebrew, they are known as *sufganiyot*, and have been universally enjoyed as a Hanukkah treat since the 1920s. (Incidentally, these are typically filled not with jelly, but with a fine-textured jam that is sometimes thickened with the help of cornstarch.)

Austria's Linzer torte is made with an almond pastry and typically filled with raspberry jam before being topped with a latticework crust. The oldest-known written recipe for this traditional pastry dates back to the 1600s, but it continues to be made both by professional confectioners and home cooks in Europe and North America.

A beloved English classic is the Victoria sponge. Named in honour of Queen Victoria, it is a sublimely simple confection consisting of rich cream and jam (generally raspberry or strawberry) between two layers of airy, sponge-like cake. A simpler variation is the Victoria Sandwich, cut into demure fingers and served without the cream. Also loved is the classic and decorative trifle, a dessert made in layers of biscuit, jam or jelly, custard and cream.

With the dawn of the new millennium, the pendulum began to swing back to earlier practices. As increasingly large segments of the global population gained access to the Internet throughout the 1990s, a new way of sharing cooking knowledge was created. The term 'blog' (from 'weblog', meaning an online personal journal) was born in 1999, and within ten years cooking blogs had proliferated, especially in the u.s. and Canada. Scores of home cooks began to blog about their kitchen experiences, and home canners made up a significant portion of these.

It would be difficult to say whether food blogs were a celebration of the newly available web technology or an

Jam- or jelly-filled doughnuts are popular around the world. These are the Polish version, known as *paczki*.

Austria's beloved jam-filled Linzer torte from the renowned Linz bakery of Leo Jindrak.

Victoria sponge, a classic jam-filled cake.

indication that people were already seeking out non-electronic activities in a reaction against constant connectivity. Probably it was a combination of both factors. The advent of 'Web 2.0', which gave users more ways to communicate online, only encouraged the phenomenon, with the inauguration of Facebook and Flickr in 2004, YouTube in 2005, Twitter in 2006 and Instagram in 2010.

Over the same period, a worldwide economic slowdown drew many people back to thrifty practices like food preserving in numbers that hadn't been seen since the end of the Second World War. The Neilsen Company reported that 'canning supplies' had become best-selling u.s. consumer goods between 2007 and 2009,[1] and a concurrent explosion of interest in 'local' foods bolstered the trend.

City-dwellers rediscovered the skills of their grandparents' generation, and urban jam-makers even started to swell the ranks of competitors at county fairs and other contests of jamming and jellying prowess. The timing was fortuitous for Jane Hasell-McCosh, who founded the World's Original Marmalade Awards and Festival in 2005. Held every March at Dalemain Mansion, a historic house in Cumbria, its 2018 edition attracted 3,000 jars from more than thirty countries. (Victoria Singh of Col. Sudhir Farm in Kota, Rajasthan, India, was the prize winner in that year's Commonwealth category.)

After a few years of writing for free, most bloggers moved on to other pursuits, but some built careers out of the movement. In San Francisco, writer Sean Timberlake until recently administered an aggregator site called Punk Domestics. From 2010 to 2018 it disseminated writing about home food preservation from a wide community of contributors. In Toronto, Joel MacCharles and Dana Harrison of the food-preserving blog Well Preserved, which launched in 2008, published more than 1,800 articles and seven hundred recipes before releasing a well-received cookbook called *Batch* in 2016.

But the doyenne of food canning and preservation blogs is Philadelphia's Marisa McClellan, whose Food in Jars has become a primary occupation. It has attracted hundreds of thousands of readers since it launched in 2009; in 2012, McClellan published her first book, *Food in Jars: Preserving in Small Batches Year Round*. She has since then released three more.

All these factors have combined to bring about a second, related phenomenon: an astonishing explosion of small, local, artisanal preserve producers, who sell their wares through farmers' markets, fine food shops and online portals. While the fruit-preserving companies that were founded as family businesses in the nineteenth century have largely been absorbed into gigantic multinational corporations, these new entrepreneurs suggest that we may be at the beginning of a second cycle that will see today's small producers grow bigger, perhaps eventually to become the beloved national brands of tomorrow.

Fruit preserves are no longer survival foods, but their history is rich with cultural allusions and individual associations. They have been gifts for royalty, nourishment for invalids, creators of employment, a cordial welcome for guests and a comfort in times of distress. Above all, the making and eating of jams, jellies and marmalades have been a means for families and communities to share customs, traditions, skills and memories, and as such they take a noble place among the culinary traditions of the world.

Recipes

IMPORTANT NOTE: The understanding of food safety has improved over the years, and some preserving methods of the past are no longer considered safe. Anyone attempting to use the recipes listed here should keep their preserves refrigerated until use, and discard any that exhibit signs of spoilage. Consult a reputable cookbook published in the current millennium for instructions on putting up preserves for long shelf storage.

Ut mala cydonia diu serventur
(That Quinces May Be Used for a Long Time)
from *Apicius*, or *De re coquinaria* (About Cooking), first century AD, Rome

This is among the earliest-known instructions for preserving fruit; already, the writer understands that if the stems are removed or the skins are damaged, the imperfect fruit may spoil and ruin the batch. *Defritum* is concentrated grape juice.

> *Eligis mala sine vitio cum ramulis et foliis, et condes in vas, et suffundes mel et defritum, et diu servabis.*
>
> Pick out unblemished quinces with stems and leaves, and place them in a vessel, and cover them with honey and defritum, and you'll be able to use them for a long time.

To Make Conserve of Quinces
after the Manner of Spaine
from A. W., *A Book of Cookrye: Very Necessary
for All Such as Delight Therin* (1591)

Egg whites (and shells) have been used for centuries, as they are here, to clear the scum from syrups and stocks.

> Take six or seven pound of Quinces, and two gallons and a halfe of water, and set your water on the fire till it be thorow warm, then put therto the whites of two Egs, shels and all, and all to stir it with a stick, and then let it stand upon the fire till it cast a great scum. Then take of the said scum, and put therto five pound of Sugar, and let it stand till it be molten, and a little while after, and then take it from the fire, and let it run through a woollen cloth of Cotten, and then put in your Quinces clean pared and the cores clean taken out, and so set them upon the fier the space of an houre and a halfe, and then take it of the fier, and strain them through a canvas cloth water and al, and then set them upon the fire again & let them seethe the space of two houres & a half, and all that time stir it with stickes with broade endes, and to know when it is inough, lay it upon a box lid, and when it commeth up cleane it is enough.

Quidini of Quinces
from Hugh Plat, *Delightes for Ladies to Adorne Their Persons, Tables,
Closets, and Distillatories: with Beauties, Banquets, Perfumes and Waters*
(1600)

Pectin-rich fruits like quinces and gooseberries turn brick-red when heated with sugar. This recipe notes that the cook can judge the cooking time by the colour of the quinces. The drop on the saucer-bottom is a test (still used) of sufficient gelling.

Take the kernells out of eight great Quinces, and boile
them in a quart of spring water, till it come to a pinte,
then put into it a quarter of a pinte of Rosewater, and one
pound of fine Sugar, and so let it boile till you see it come
to bee of a deepe colour: then take a drop, and drop it
on the bottome of a sawcer, then let it run through a gelly
bagge into a bason, then set it in your bason upon a
chafing dish of coles to keep it warm, then take a spoone,
and fill your boxes as full as you please, and when they
be colde cover them: and if you please to printe it in
moldes, you must have moldes made to the bigness of
your boxe, and wet your moldes with Rosewater, and so
let it run into your mold, and when it is colde turne it off
into your boxes. If you wette your moldes with water,
your gelly will fall out of them.

To Make Suckets
from Gervase Markham, *The English Huswife* (1615)

These suckets consist of a fruit paste moulded into the fruit rinds,
which can be cut into wedges when set. These decorative, multi-
coloured jellies in citrus shells make an attractive presentation,
and were a common feature of the Georgian dessert table. Letting jam or jelly 'fall from the spoon' is another still-used test
of sufficient gelling; when the mixture 'sheets' off the spoon in
thick blobs rather than dripping off like syrup, it is done. 'Pom-
ecitron' is the citron or etrog. 'Swinge' is another word for 'beat'.
'Sweet wort' is the liquid from malted grain before hops are added
in beer brewing. The term 'walm' is an obsolete word meaning
'bubble up'.

Take curds, the parings of lemons, of oranges or pom-
ecitrons, or indeed any half ripe green fruit, and boil
them till they be tender, in sweet wort, then make a syrip
in this sort: take three pound of sugar, and the whites of
four eggs, and a gallon of water; then swinge and beat the

water and the eggs together, and then put in your sugar, and set it on the fire, and let it have an easy fire, and so let it boil six or seven walms, and then strain it through a cloth, and let it seethe again till it fall from the spoon, and then put it into the rinds of fruits.

To Make Paste of Apricocks
from W. M., *The Queens Closet Opened* (1658)

This recipe makes an apricot paste that is then decoratively moulded back into the shape of whole apricots. Today, we know when sugar has reached 'candy height', otherwise known as the 'pearl' or 'soft ball' stage, when it has reached 105°C (220°F), according to a sugar thermometer.

Take your Apricocks, and pare them, and stone them, then boil them tender betwixt two dishes on a Chafing dish of coals, then being cold, lay it forth on a white sheet of paper; then take as much Sugar as it doth weigh and boil it to a Candy height, with as much Rose-water and fair water as will melt the Sugar; and so let it boil till it be as thick as for marmalet, now and then stirring of it; then fashion it upon a Pie-plate like to half Apricocks, and the next day close the half Apricocks to the other, and when they are dry, they will be as clear as Amber, and eat much better then Apricocks it self.

Cotignac espais (Firm Cotignac)
from *Le Confiturier François,* attributed to François la Varenne (1664)

'Pearl sugar' may refer to the coarsely ground product now known as 'preserving' sugar. The term today refers to a hard, seed-like product used in some Scandinavian baked goods, and to top Belgian waffles.

Pelez des coings bien murs, coupés-les par morceaux, faites les bien cuire dans l'eau, & puis apres les passez dans une passoire bien deliée, prenez ce qui sera passé, faites cuire du sucre à perle avec de l'eau dans laquelle auront cuit les coings, faites les boüiller à petit feu iusqu'à ce qu'ils soient cuits en gelée, & les serrez dans les boëtes de sapin. Il faut à une livre de marmelade une livre de sucre.
Peel well ripened quinces, cut them into pieces, cook them well in water and then pass them through a coarse sieve, take what has passed through, cook pearl sugar in the water the quinces were cooked in, and boil it over a low fire until they gel, and seal them in pine boxes. One pound of marmalade takes one pound of sugar.

To Make Raspberry Paste
from John Nott, *The Cooks and Confectioners Dictionary; or, The Accomplish'd Housewifes Companion* (1723)

These confections are cut into shapes; from this type of recipe, we have inherited modern fruit gums and jelly/gummy candies.

Strain Raspberries hard through a Cloth, boil the Juice, for each Pound of Juice take a Pound of double-refin'd Sugar, and as much fair Water as will wet it, boil them to a Candy Height, i.e. till it will lie upon a Plate clear, like a chrystal Drop; then put it into the Raspberry Juice, stirring it continually 'till the Juice and Sugar be well mix'd, set it on the Fire, and let it have a Walm or two, and so put it into Glasses for Paste, scarcely an Inch thick, put it on a Stone where it may be but warm; and when it is grown stiff enough to cut, turn it our upon glaz'd Paper, and cut it into what Forms you please, then lay them on the Stone again, and dry them up.

Moon-shine

from Hannah Glasse, *The Art of Cookery Made Plain and Easy* (1747),
2nd edn

This recipe is delightfully whimsical; the result will be a dish of
almond-flavoured blancmange with inset jelly stars and moons. (If
she were alive today, Hannah Glasse would no doubt be a major
figure on Instagram.)

First have a Piece of Tin made in the Shape of a Half-
Moon as deep as a Half-pint Bason, and one in the Shape
of a large Star, and two or three lesser ones. Boil two
Calf's Feet in a Gallon of Water till it comes to a Quart,
then strain it off, and when cold skim off all the Fat, take
Half the Jelly and sweeten it with Sugar to your Palate,
beat up the Whites of four Eggs, stir all together over a
slow Fire till it boils, then run it through a Flannel Bag
till clear, put it in a clean Sauce-Pan, and take an Ounce
of sweet Almonds blanched and beat very fin in a Marble
Mortar, with two Spoonfuls of thick Cream, stir it all
together till it boils, then have ready the Dish you intend
it for, lay the Tin in the Shape of a Half-Moon in the
Middle, and the Stars around it; lay little Weights on the
Tin to keep them in the Places you would have them lye,
then pour in the above *Blanc Manger* into the Dish, and
when it is quite cold take out the Tin Things, and mix
the other Half of the Jelly with Half a Pint of good White
Wine and the Juice of two or three Lemons, with Loaf-
sugar enough to make it sweet, and the Whites of eight
Eggs beat fine; stir it all together over a slow Fire till it
boils, then run it through a Flannel Bag till it is quite
clear into a China Bason, and very carefully fill up the
Places where you took the Tin out; let it stand till cold,
and send it to the Table.

Note: You may for change fill the Dish with a fine
thick Almond Custard, and when it is cool fill up the
Half-Moon and Stars with the clear Jelly.

To Make Currant Jelly

from Hannah Glasse, *The Art of Cookery Made Plain and Easy* (1758),
6th edn

Strip the currants from the stalks, put them in a Stone Jar, stop it
close, set it in a Kettle of boiling Water half-way the Jar, let it boil
half an Hour, take it out and strain the Juice thro' a coarse Hair-
sieve; to a Pint of Juice put a Pound of Sugar, set it over a fine quick
clear Fire in your Preserving-pan or Bell-metal Skillet; keep stirring
it all the Time till the Sugar is melted, then skim the Scum off as
fast as it rises. When your Jelly is very clear and fine, pour it into
Gallipots; when cold, cut white Paper just the Bigness of the Top
of the Pot and lay on the Jelly, dip those Papers in Brandy, then
cover the Top close with white Paper, and prick it full of Holes;
set it in a dry Place, put some into Glasses, and paper them.

To Make Raspberry Giam

from Hannah Glasse, *The Art of Cookery Made Plain and Easy* (1758),
6th edn

The currant jelly from the previous recipe is here used to set the
raspberries, which are weak in pectin. Note the archaic spelling
of 'jam'.

> Take a pint of this Currant Jelly, and a Quart of Rasp-
> berries, bruise them well together, set them over a slow
> Fire, keeping them stirring all the Time till it boils. Let it
> boil five or six Minutes, and pour it into your Gallipots,
> paper as you do the Currant Jelly, and keep for Use. They
> will keep two or three Years, and have the full Flavour
> of the Raspberry.

A Short Paste for Tarts
from Elizabeth Moxon, *English Housewifry* (1764)

This pastry recipe, flavoured with rosewater, as was common at the time, is delicious and fool-proof. The tart shells can be filled with any type of jam.

> Take a Pound of Wheat-flower, and rub it very small, three Quarters of a Pound of Butter, rub it as small as the Flower, put to it three Spoonfuls of Loaf Sugar beat and sifted, take the Yolks of four Eggs, and beat them very well; put to them a Spoonful or two of Rose-Water, and work them into a Paste, then roll them thin, and Ice them over as you did the other if you please, and bake them in a slow Oven.

To Know When Your Sugar is at Candy Height
from Elizabeth Moxon, *English Housewifry* (1764)

> Take some Sugar and clarify it till it come to a candy Height, and keep it still boiling till it become thick, then stir it with a Stick from you, and when it is at candy Height it will fly from your Stick like Flakes of Snow, or Feathers flying in the Air, and till it comes to that Height it will not fly, then you may use it as you please.

Raspberry Puffs
from Mary Smith, *The Complete House-keeper
and Professed Cook* (1786)

'Puffs' are equivalent to turnovers.

> Roll out some puff-paste, cut it in pieces three inches square, put on a little raspberry-jam, wet it round the edges, and close up, the one half over the other, do it

over with egg, and bake them of a nice brown; seven are enough for a dish; and serve them up for a second course, or for supper.

Strawberry Jam
from A Person (Frederick Nutt), *The Complete Confectioner; or, The Whole Art of Confectionary* (1789)

A 'spaddle' is literally a little spade, so, here, a flat-edged spoon. Today 'powdered sugar' often means the very fine confectioner's sugar; in this context, it simply means granulated sugar.

Pick the stalks from the strawberries, and put them into a large copper preserving pan, mash them with your spaddle to break them as much as you can; put them over the fire, make them quite hot almost to boil; pass them through a very fine cullender, boil the strawberries you have passed twenty minutes, stirring them all the time with your spaddle; weight your strawberries and allow fifteen ounces of powdered sugar to every pound of strawberries; put in the sugar and boil them together, stirring them from the bottom (else they will burn) for half an hour over the fire; fill your pans and sift some powdered sugar on the tops of them before you put them by, and the next day put papers over them.

Gooseberry Jam for Tarts
from Maria Rundell, *A New System of Domestic Cookery* (1814)

Put twelve pounds of the red hairy gooseberries, when ripe and gathered in dry weather, into a preserving-pan, with a pint of currant juice, drawn as for jelly; let them boil pretty quick, and beat them with the spoon; when they begin to break, put to them six pounds of pure white sugar, and simmer slowly to a jam. It requires long boiling,

or will not keep; but is an excellent and reasonable things
for tarts or puffs. Look at it in two or three days, and if
the syrup and fruit separate, the whole must be boiled
longer. Be careful it does not burn to the bottom.

Apple Pudding with Pistachio Nuts
from Richard Dolby, *The Cook's Dictionary,
and House-keeper's Directory: A New Family Manual* (1830)

Peel thirty renneting apples, cut them in quarters, and
then cut each quarter into four or five pieces. Then put
them into a stew-pan with six ounces of fine sugar (over
which should be grated the rind of a lemon) four ounces
of butter, lukewarm, four ounces of green pistachio nuts
(whole), and rather more than half a pot of apricot marmalade; let them stew till they are warmed through,
then pour them into a dish. Prepare your paste, line your
mould, put in your apples . . . When it is ready to serve,
mask it with apricot marmalade, and strew pistachio nuts,
chopped small, over it.

Preserves, &c.
from Mrs (Lydia) Child, *The American Frugal Housewife*,
16th edn (1836), USA

Possibly the grumpiest preserving recipe ever published, Mrs
Child's instructions show that the medicinal use of fruit preserves
persisted well into the nineteenth century. Her extreme thriftiness
is evident in her casual instruction simply to reheat preserves that
have started to spoil.

Economical people will seldom use preserves, except for
sickness. They are unhealthy, expensive, and useless to
those who are well. Barberries preserved in molasses
are very good for common use. Boil the molasses, skim

it, throw in the barberries, and simmer them till they are soft. If you wish to lay by a few for sickness, preserve them in sugar by the same rule as other preserves. Melt the sugar, skim it, throw in the barberries; when done soft, take them out, and throw in others.

A pound of sugar to a pound of fruit is the rule for all preserves. The sugar should be melted over a fire moderate enough not to scorch it. When melted, it should be skimmed clean, and the fruit dropped in to simmer till it is soft. Plums, and things of which the skin is liable to be broken, do better to be put in little jars, with their weight of sugar, and the jars set in a kettle of boiling water, till the fruit is done. See the water is not so high as to boil into the jars.

When you put preserves in jars, lay a white paper, thoroughly wet with brandy, flat upon the surface of the preserves, and cover them carefully from the air. If they begin to mould, scald them by setting them in the oven till boiling hot. Glass is much better than earthen for preserves; they are not half as apt to ferment.

Bakewell Pudding (Very Rich)
from Mrs (Isabella) Beeton, *The Book of Household Management* (1859–61)

110 g (¼ lb) of puff-paste [puff pastry]
5 eggs
170 g (6 oz) sugar
110 g (¼ lb) butter
30 g (1 oz) almonds
jam

Mode. – Cover a dish with thin paste, and put over this a layer of any kind of jam, ½ inch [1.25 cm] thick; put the yolks of 5 eggs into a basin with the white of 1, and beat these well; add the sifted sugar, the butter, which should be melted, and the almonds, which should be well pounded; beat all together until well mixed, then pour it into the dish over the jam, and bake for an hour in a moderate oven.

Time. – 1 hour. Average cost, 1s. 6d.

Sufficient for 4 or 6 persons. Seasonable at any time.

Orange Marmalade 1
from Mrs (Isabella) Beeton, *The Book of Household Management*
(1859–61)

This recipe calls for discarding the water in which the orange rinds are boiled, wasting useful pectin content. Pigs' bladders or paper brushed with egg-white are used to seal the pots.

Ingredients. – Equal weight of fine loaf sugar and Seville oranges; to 12 oranges allow 560 ml (1 pint) of water.

Mode. – Let there be an equal weight of loaf sugar and Seville oranges, and allow the above proportion of water to every dozen oranges. Peel them carefully, remove a little of the white pith, and boil the rinds in water 2 hours, changing the water three times to take off a little of the bitter taste. Break the pulp into small pieces, take out all the pips, and cut the boiled rind into chips. Make a syrup with the sugar and water; boil this well, skim it, and, when clear, put in the pulp and chips. Boil all together from 20 minutes to ½ hour; pour it into pots, and, when cold, cover down with bladders or tissue-paper brushed over on both sides with the white of an egg. The juice and grated rind of 2 lemons to every dozen of oranges, added with the pulp and chips to the syrup, are a very great improvement to this marmalade.

Time. – 2 hours to boil the orange-rinds; 10 minutes to boil the syrup; 20 minutes to ½ hour to boil the marmalade.

Average cost, from 6d. to 8d. per lb. pot.

Seasonable. – This should be made in March or April, as Seville oranges are then in perfection.

Apple Porcupine
from Mary Johnson Bailey Lincoln,
*Mrs Lincoln's Boston Cook Book: What to Do
and What Not to Do in Cooking* (1884)

Arrange eight or ten apples (baked as in the preceding rule, or cored, pared, and cooked carefully in syrup . . .) in a mound on a dish for serving. Put quince jelly among the apples. Cover with a meringue made of the whites of four eggs and half a cup of powdered sugar. Stick blanched almonds into the meringue. Put the dish on a board in the oven, and brown slightly, or hold a hot iron over it. Serve with boiled custard sauce.

Currant Jelly
from Fannie Farmer, *The Boston Cooking-school
Cook Book* (1896)

Currants are in the best condition for making jelly between June twenty-eighth and July third, and should not be picked directly after a rain. Cherry currants make the best jelly. Equal proportions of red and white currants are considered desirable, and make a lighter colored jelly.

Pick over currants, but do not remove stems; wash and drain. Mash a few in the bottom of a preserving kettle, using a wooden potato masher; so continue until berries are used. Cook slowly until currants look white. Strain through a coarse strainer, then allow juice to drop through a double thickness of cheese-cloth or a jelly bag. Measure, bring to boiling-point, and boil five minutes; add an equal measure of heated sugar, boil three minutes, skim, and pour into glasses. Place in a sunny window, and let stand twenty-four hours. Cover, and keep in a cool, dry place.

Grape Jelly

from Fannie Farmer, *The Boston Cooking-School Cook Book* (1896)

Grapes should be picked over, washed, and stems removed before putting into a preserving kettle. Heat to boiling-point, mash, and boil thirty minutes; then proceed as for Currant Jelly. Wild grapes make the best jelly.

Rowan Jelly

from *The Edinburgh Book of Plain Cookery Recipes*, prepared for the Edinburgh College of Domestic Science, 1932

Rowan jelly is traditionally served with Twelfth Night Cake in England. The rowan is better known as the mountain ash in North America; its berries are somewhat toxic until they have been frozen either naturally or in the freezer.

Wash the berries. Put into a preserving pan. Cover with cold water and cook to a pulp. Strain. To each pint of warm juice allow one pound of sugar. Bring to boiling-point. Cook for about twenty minutes. Test, skim, and pour into small pots.

Crushed Strawberry Jam

from *Economy Recipes for Canada's "Housoldiers"* by the Canada Starch Company, 1943

This recipe was issued in a wartime recipe booklet published by the makers of Crown Brand Corn Syrup, so it not only shows home cooks how to save their rationed sugar, but touts Crown

Brand's own product. Note the use of liquid pectin to ensure a firm set of a fruit that has little natural pectin.

2.25 l (2 quarts/8 cups) whole, cleaned strawberries
(1 l/1 quart/4 cups crushed)
700 g (3 ½ cups) sugar
800 g (2⅓ cups) Crown Brand Corn Syrup
½ bottle liquid pectin

Wash and hull berries. Mash well; mix with sugar and Crown Brand Syrup in preserving kettle. Bring slowly to a boil and boil hard for 10 to 15 minutes, stirring frequently. Remove from fire, stir in pectin; stir and skim. Pour into hot, sterilized glasses and seal. Store in a cool, dark, dry place. *Yield:* 10 glasses (170 ml/6 fl. oz.)

A Simple Serviceberry Jam Recipe
adapted from the blog Eat Locally. Blog Globally.
by Sarah B. Hood, 2013

700 g (1.5 lb) serviceberries (which are the same as saskatoon berries)
700 g (1.5 lb) sugar
60 ml (¼ cup) lemon juice

Combine all the ingredients in a large, non-reactive pot. Cook over medium-high heat, stirring frequently to help the steam escape quickly. When it reaches the setting point, you can seal and process in jars or just refrigerate. This makes quite a sweet jam, and there will be those who don't like the seeds. However, if you let it stay on the stove long enough to be really sure, the set's fantastic. If you like a tarter jam, reduce the sugar to one pound and perhaps add an extra couple of tablespoons of lemon juice. *Makes about 800 g (2½ cups)*

Tomato Jam

from Marisa McClellan, *The Food in Jars Kitchen: 140 Ways to Cook, Bake, Plate, and Share Your Homemade Pantry* (2019) (reprinted with permission of the author)

Several summers ago my friend Amy gave me a jar of tomato jam with the recipe attached and now I can't go back to a life without it. I use it in place of ketchup, as well as in places where ketchup wouldn't dare to tread. (Try it with a soft, stinky cheese. It is life-changing.) For those of you who are accustomed to preserving tomatoes, you'll notice that this recipe does not call for you to first peel them. This is not a mistake. The first time I made it, I thought I could improve on things and peeled and seeded the tomatoes prior to cooking them down. However, without those bits, the finished jam was too sweet and entirely without texture. It needs the skin and seeds to keep things interesting.

2.3 kg (5 lb) tomatoes, cored and finely chopped
700 g (3½ cups) granulated sugar
120 ml (½ cup) freshly squeezed lime juice
2 teaspoons grated peeled fresh ginger
1 teaspoon ground cinnamon
½ teaspoon ground cloves
1 tablespoon sea salt
1 tablespoon red pepper flakes

Combine all ingredients in a large, non-reactive pot. Bring to a boil over high heat and then reduce the heat to medium. Cook the jam at a low boil, stirring regularly, until it reduces to a sticky, jammy mess. This will take 1½–2 hours. When the jam is nearly done, prepare a boiling water bath and 4 regular-mouth 500 ml/1-pint jars.

When the jam has cooked down sufficiently, remove the pot from the heat and ladle it into the prepared jars. Wipe the rims, apply the lids and rings, and process in a boiling water bath for 20 minutes.

Makes 4 (500 ml/1 pint) jars

References

1 Preserving Traditions

1 Melissa A. Click and Ronit Ridberg, 'Saving Food: Food Preservation as Alternative Food Activism', *Environmental Communication*, IV/3 (September 2010), pp. 301–17.

2 Roman and Persian Contributions

1 Najmieh Batmanglij, *A Taste of Persia* (London, 2007), p. 165.
2 Jamshedji Maneckji Unvala, trans., 'King Husrav and his Boy' by Khusrau i Kavātān (Paris, n.d.), accessed online via Hathi Trust Digital Library at www.hathitrust.org, accessed 20 January 2011.
3 As quoted in Forough-es-Saltanah Hekmat, *The Art of Persian Cooking* (New York, 1961), p. 18.
4 Nawal Nasrallah, trans. and ed., *Annals of the Caliphs' Kitchens: Ibn Sayyār al-Warrāq's Tenth-century Baghdadi Cookbook* (Boston, MA, 2007), pp. 392, 484–7, 597, 599, 625, 748.
5 Elizabeth Abbott, *Sugar: A Bittersweet History* (Toronto, 2008), p. 21.
6 Susan Pinkard, *A Revolution in Taste: The Rise of French Cuisine* (Cambridge, 2009), pp. 19–20.

3 Elaborate Banqueting Dishes: The 1500s

1 James Hart quoted in Elizabeth Abbott, *Sugar: A Bittersweet History* (Toronto, 2008), p. 15.
2 C. M. Woolgar, *The Culture of Food in England, 1200–1500* (New Haven, CT, 2016), pp. 98–9.

4 Sweet Confections to End the Meal: The 1600s

1 Peter Mcinnis, *The Story of Sugar* (Crows Nest, NSW, Australia, 2002), p. 81.
2 'Manufacture of Bar-le-Duc Jelly', *Journal of the Royal Society of Arts*, LXIV/33 (27 October 1916), accessed at http://www.jstor.org.
3 Olive M. Geddes, *The Laird's Kitchen: Three Hundred Years of Food in Scotland* (Edinburgh, 1994), pp. 17c20.

5 Elegant Desserts and Breakfast Preserves: The 1700s

1 Susan Pinkard, *A Revolution in Taste: The Rise of French Cuisine* (Cambridge, 2009), p. 149.
2 Stephan Guyenet, 'By 2606, the U.S. Diet will be 100 Percent Sugar', *Whole Health Source* (18 February 2012), accessed at http://wholehealthsource.blogspot.ca. U.S. per capita consumption of sugar rose drastically over the course of the next two centuries, of course, peaking at 107.7 lb (48.9 kg) per person in 1999.
3 Elizabeth David, *Is There a Nutmeg in the House?* (London, 2000), pp. 237–8.
4 Dan Cruickshank, *The Secret History of Georgian London: How the Wages of Sin Shaped the Capital* (London, 2009), pp. 225, 232.

6 Recipes for Home Cooks: The 1800s

1 Sidney Wilfred Mintz, *Sweetness and Power: The Place of Sugar in Modern History* (New York, 1986), p. 118.

2 Richard Sterling, Kate Reeves and Georgia Dacakis, *Lonely Planet World Food: Greece* (Melbourne, 2002), p. 77.

3 Diane Kochilas, 'A Short History of Spoon Sweets', www.dianekochilas.com, 18 June 2012.

4 Andrew and Rachel Dalby, *Gifts from the Gods: A History of Food in Greece* (London, 2017), p. 252.

5 George Wheler, *A Journey into Greece* (London, 1682), p. 458.

6 Quoted in Dalby and Dalby, *Gifts of the Gods*, p. 253.

7 Helen and Billie, 'Quince Spoon Sweet (Κυδώνι γλυκό του κουταλιού)', https://miakouppa.com, 20 November 2017.

8 Darra Goldstein, 'It's Berry Time!', *Russian Life*, XLVI/4 (July–August 2003), accessed at www.questia.com.

9 Benjamin Shinewald, 'Jews in Canada: Sweet Preservation', www.winnipegfreepress.com, 3 December 2015.

7 Ventures in Commercial Marmalade

1 'Animus, Absenteeism, and Succession in the Keiller Marmalade Dynasty, 1839–1919', *Journal of Scottish Historical Studies*, XXXVII/1 (2008), p. 44.

2 Ibid., p. 59.

3 Kirsty Hooper, 'Oranges Are the Only Fruit: John Moir & Sons (Aberdeen, London and Seville) and the Re-Hispanicizing of Marmalade', *Hispanic Britain; or, An Anglo-Spanish Miscellany* (30 October 2013), accessed at https://hispanicbritain.wordpress.com.

8 A Great Jam-factory Explosion: Victorian Entrepreneurs

1 Peter J. Atkins, 'Vinegar and Sugar: The Early History of Factory-made Jams, Pickles and Sauces in Britain', *The Food Industries of Europe in the Nineteenth and Twentieth Centuries*, ed. Alain Drouard (Abingdon-on-Thames, 2016), p. 46.
2 See Nigel Jeffries, Lyn Blackmore and David Sorapure, *Crosse and Blackwell, 1830–1921: A British Food Manufacturer in London's West End* (London, 2016).
3 Atkins, 'Vinegar and Sugar', p. 47.
4 Ibid., p. 50.
5 Nicholas Hartley, *Bittersweet: The Story of Hartley's Jam* (Amberley, Gloucestershire, 2011), p. 92. 'White slave' in this case was not a reference to women abducted into prostitution, but a term being used by social reformers to refer to the disempowered working class.
6 Ibid., pp. 46–7.

9 The Workers Boil Over: Labour Unrest in Edwardian London

1 J. H. Treble, cThe Seasonal Demand for Adult Labour in Glasgow, 1890–1914', *Social History*, III/1 (January 1978), p. 58, accessed at www.jstor.org.
2 Helen Bosanquet, 'A Study in Women's Wages', *Economic Journal*, XII/45 (March 1902), pp. 42–3.
3 Peter J. Atkins, 'Vinegar and Sugar: The Early History of Factory-made Jams, Pickles and Sauces in Britain', *The Food Industries of Europe in the Nineteenth and Twentieth Centuries*, ed. Alain Drouard (Abingdon-on-Thames, 2016), p. 49.
4 Amanda Wilkinson, 'J is for Jam Maker', 10 March 2016, http://victorianoccupations.co.uk.
5 Thomas Farrell, 'The Fruit of Enterprise: Pink's Jam', http://letslookagain.com, 11 July 2015.

6 George Dangerfield, *The Strange Death of Liberal England* (London, 1936), p. 254.

7 Ibid., p. 255.

8 Farrell, 'The Fruit of Enterprise'.

10 International Condiment Empires

1 Nicholas Hartley, *Bittersweet: The Story of Hartley's Jam* (Amberley, Gloucestershire, 2011), p. 147.

2 Betty O'Brien, 'The Lord's Supper: Fruit of the Vine or Cup of Devils?', *Methodist History*, xxxi/4 (July 1993), pp. 218–19.

11 Offerings from the Home Front: Wartime Preserving

1 Sue Shepherd, *Pickled, Potted and Canned: The Story of Food Preserving* (London, 2000), p. 329.

2 Charles Batey, *The History of the Women's Institute Movement of England and Wales* (Oxford, 1953), pp. 115–16.

3 Mildred Summers, 'Jam for Britain', *Canadian Red Cross Despatch* (June–July 1944), p. 8.

4 Peter Lockyer, 'An Uncertain Harvest: Hard Work, Big Business and Changing Times in Prince Edward County, Ontario', *Material Culture Review* (1 January 1991), available at https://journals.lib.unb.ca.

12 New Voices: Jams, Jellies and Marmalades in the Twenty-first Century

1 The Neilsen Company, 'Consumers Cut Back Retail Sales Change as Value Trumps All', www.nielsen.com, 29 January 2009.

Select Bibliography

Abbott, Elizabeth, *Sugar: A Bittersweet History* (Toronto, 2008)

Astarita, Tommaso, *The Italian Baroque Tables, Cooking and Entertaining from the Golden Age of Naples* (Tempe, AZ, 2004)

Atkins, Peter J., 'Vinegar and Sugar: The Early History of Factory-made Jams, Pickles and Sauces in Britain', *The Food Industries of Europe in the Nineteenth and Twentieth Centuries*, ed. Alain Drouard (Abingdon-on-Thames, 2016)

Benham, Maura, *The Story of Tiptree Jam: The First Hundred Years* (Tiptree, 1983)

Black, Clementina, ed., *Married Women's Work* (London, 1915), accessed at https://archive.org

Bosanquet, Helen, 'A Study in Women's Wages', *Economic Journal*, XII/45 (March 1902), pp. 42–9.

Brears, Peter, *Cooking and Dining in Tudor and Early Stuart England* (London, 2015)

—, *Jellies and Their Moulds* (Devon, 2010)

'Chivers & Sons Ltd., Souvenir of the Orchard Factory', *c.* 1923, Histon, Cambridge, reproduced at https://histonandimpingtonvillagesociety.wordpress.com

Dalby, Andrew and Rachel, *Gifts of the Gods: A Global History of Food in Greece* (London, 2017)

De la Mare, Ursula, 'Necessity and Rage: The Factory Women's Strikes in Bermondsey, 1911', *History Workshop Journal*, 66 (Autumn 2008), pp. 62–80, accessed at www.jstor.org

Duerr, A. N., K. Boswick and A. Collinson, *The Story of F. Duerr & Sons, 1881–2016*, 6th edn (Manchester, 2016)

Geddes, Olive M., *The Laird's Kitchen: Three Hundred Years of Food in Scotland* (Edinburgh, 1994)

Hartley, Nicholas, *Bittersweet: The Story of Hartley's Jam* (Stroud, 2011)

Jeffries, Nigel, Lyn Blackmore and David Sorapure, *Crosse and Blackwell, 1830–1921: A British Food Manufacturer in London's West End*, Crossrail Archaeology Series (London, 2016)

Laszlo, Pierre, *Citrus: A History* (Chicago, IL, 2007)

Mcinnis, Peter, *Bittersweet: The Story of Sugar* (Crows Nest, NSW, 2002)

McIver, Katherine, *Kitchens: Cooking and Eating in Medieval Italy* (London, 2017)

Markham, Gervase, *The English Huswife* (London, 1615)

'Marmalade', *Scientific American*, XVII/18 (2 November 1867), p. 277, accessed at www.jstor.org

Mathew, W. M., 'Animus, Absenteeism, and Succession in the Keiller Marmalade Dynasty, 1839–1919', *Journal of Scottish Historical Studies*, XXVIII/1 (2008), pp. 44–61

—, *The Secret History of Guernsey Marmalade: James Keiller and Son Offshore, 1857–1879* (St Peter Port, 1998)

Mazumdar, Sucheta, *Sugar and Society in China: Peasants, Technology, and the World Market* (Cambridge, MA, 1998)

Mintz, Sidney Wilfred, *Sweetness and Power: The Place of Sugar in Modern History* (New York, 1986)

Pinkard, Susan, *A Revolution in Taste: The Rise of French Cuisine* (Cambridge, 2009)

Quellier, Florent, *La Table des français: Une histoire culturelle (XVe—début XIXXe siècle)* (Rennes, 2007)

Shepherd, Sue, *Pickled, Potted and Canned: The Story of Food Preserving* (London, 2000)

Sim, Alison, *Food and Feast in Tudor England* (Stroud, 2005)

Smith, Andrew F., *Sugar: A Global History* (London, 2015)

Wilson, C. Anne, *The Book of Marmalade* (Totnes, 2010)

Woolgar, C. M., *The Culture of Food in England, 1200–1500* (New Haven, CT, 2016)

Websites and Associations

Bompas & Parr
www.bompasandparr.com

Chivers
www.chivers.ie

Concord Grape Association
www.concordgrape.org

E. D. Smith
www.edsmith.com

Federated Women's Institutes of Canada (FWIC)
www.fwic.ca

Food in Jars
www.foodinjars.com

Grace's Guide to British Industrial History
www.gracesguide.co.uk

Hain Daniels Group
www.haindaniels.com

Hero Group
www.hero-group.ch

The J. M. Smucker Company
www.smuckers.com

Les Produits cotignacs d'Orléans
www.cducentre.com/produit-cotignacs_orleans

Let's Look Again: A History of Branded Britain
http://letslookagain.com

Литературный Варе́нье (Literary Varenye)
http://litvarenie.ru

Mia Kouppa
miakouppa.com

Moir's
www.moirs.co.za

Moorehouse History
www.moorhousehistory.co.uk

National Center for Home Food Preservation
https://nchfp.uga.edu

Robertson's
www.robertsons.co.uk

Rose's
www.rosesmarmalade.co.uk

Welch's
www.welchs.com

Well Preserved
www.wellpreserved.ca

Wilkin & Sons
www.tiptree.com

The World's Original Marmalade Awards
www.dalemain.com

Acknowledgements

Many thanks are due to Carolyn Crawford, Sylvia Lovegren, Niamh Malcolm, Bill McAskill, Sherry Murphy, Jan Pimblett, Jonathan St Rose, Mya Sangster, Gillian Sutcliffe, Ula Zukowska, members of the Culinary Historians of Canada, participants in Toronto's Volunteer Historic Cooks programme, staff at Montgomery's Inn and Fort York National Historic Site, and my family for their ongoing assistance, support and inspiration.

Photo Acknowledgements

The author and publishers wish to express their thanks to the below sources of illustrative material and/or permission to reproduce it.

Alamy: p. 57 (Heritage Images Partnership Ltd); Bavarian State Painting Collections: p. 26 (Alte Pinakothek, Munich); Boston Public Library: p. 37; Comité Départemental du Tourisme de la Meuse, Bar-le-Duc, France: p. 27; Cooper Hewitt, Smithsonian Design Museum: p. 21 (The Robert L. Metzenberg Collection, gift of Eleanor L. Metzenberg); Flickr: p. 97 (Linda Peall); Erella Ganon; p. 56; courtesy of Joseph Glazner and Shirriff family: p. 79; Hermitage Museum, St Petersburg, Russia: p. 25; Sarah B. Hood: pp. 34, 35, 95, 98; iStockphoto: p. 6 (AlasdairJames); Niamh Malcolm: pp. 81, 96 bottom; Metropolitan Museum of Art (gift of Dr Louis R Slattery, 1980 (accession number 1980.33)): p. 17 (gift of Dr Louis R. Slattery, 1980 (accession number 1980.33)), National Gallery of Art, Washington, DC: p. 24 (Samuel H. Kress Collection); Rednersville WI, Ameliasburgh, Ontario, Canada: pp. 91, 92; courtesy of E. D. Smith Foods Ltd: p. 80; State Library Victoria, Australia: p. 78 (Henry Jones IXL collection of photographs, Gift of George Crompton); Tourism Loiret: p. 20 (© C-Mouton); TUC Library Collections at London Metropolitan University: p. 75; Wellcome Collection: pp. 14, 42; Mary F. Williamson: p. 53; U.S. Department of Agriculture, National Agricultural Library: p. 89; U.S. Food and Drug Administration: p. 87; U.S. National Archives and Records Administration: pp. 85 (National Archives at College

Park. U.S. Food Administration. Educational Division. Advertising Section.), 86 (Archives at College Park - Archives II (College Park, MD)), 88 (Department of Agriculture. Extension Service. Still Picture Records Section (College Park, MD)).

Deben Dave (public domain): p. 68; Rebecca Siegel, the copyright holder of the image on p. 18, has published it online under conditions imposed by a Creative Commons Attribution 2.0 Generic License. Jeremy Keith from Brighton and Hove, United Kingdom, the copyright holder of the image on p. 30, has published it online under conditions imposed by a Creative Commons Attribution 2.0 Generic License. Gaetan Lee: p. 99 bottom. This image, which was originally posted to Flickr, was uploaded to Wikimedia Commons using the Flickr upload bot on 22 January 2009, 19:45 by Gveret Tered. On that date, it was confirmed to be licensed under the terms of the license indicated: Creative Commons Attribution 2.0 Generic License. Dennis Jarvis from Halifax, Canada, the copyright holder of the image on p. 8, has published it online under conditions imposed by a Creative Commons Attribution-Share Alike 2.0 Generic License. Anonymous Wikipedian, the copyright holder of the image on p. 45, has published it online under conditions imposed by a Creative Commons Attribution 3.0 Unported License. Georgia About/Georgian Recipes. net, the copyright holder of the image on p. 48 top, has published it online under conditions imposed by a Creative Commons Attribution 3.0 Unported License. Moonsun1981, the copyright holder of the image on p. 48 bottom, has published it online under conditions imposed by a Creative Commons Attribution-Share Alike 3.0 Unported License. Honza Gron (Jagro), the copyright holder of the image on p. 96 top, has published it online under conditions imposed by a Creative Commons Attribution-Share Alike Unported 3.0 License. Leo Jindrak, the copyright holder of the image on p. 99 top (originally uploaded by Uwe berger), has published it online under conditions imposed by a Creative Commons Attribution-Share Alike Unported 3.0 License. Rahul rages, the copyright holder of the image on p. 13, has published it online under conditions imposed by a Creative Commons Attribution-Share Alike

Index

italic numbers refer to illustrations; **bold** to recipes